an atlas of cat anatomy

HAZEL E. FIELD

and

MARY E. TAYLOR

Scientific Illustrator

SECOND EDITION
revised and enlarged by

BERNARD B. BUTTERWORTH

THE UNIVERSITY OF CHICAGO PRESS

CHICAGO AND LONDON

Riverside Community·College
Library
4800 Magnolia Avenue
Riverside, CA 92506

THE UNIVERSITY OF CHICAGO COMMITTEE
ON PUBLICATIONS IN BIOLOGY AND MEDICINE

LESTER R. DRAGSTEDT · R. WENDELL HARRISON
FRANKLIN C. McLEAN · C. PHILLIP MILLER
THOMAS PARK · WILLIAM H. TALIAFERRO

International Standard Book Number: 0-226-24817-8

Library of Congress Catalog Card Number: 69-16998

THE UNIVERSITY OF CHICAGO PRESS, CHICAGO 60637
THE UNIVERSITY OF CHICAGO PRESS, LTD., LONDON

© *1950, 1969 by The University of Chicago. All rights re-
served. Published 1950. Second Edition 1969*
Printed in the United States of America

85 84 □ 7 6 5 4

Designed and prepared by Kottcamp & Young

PREFACE To First Edition

AN ATLAS OF CAT ANATOMY

is intended as a visual aid for the student, a teaching aid for the instructor. Its use in the laboratory will make it possible for the student to observe and read with little interruption while dissecting, and it will make it possible for the instructor to demonstrate the fundamentals of mammalian anatomy clearly and with little effort.

The text accompanying each plate is concise, and excessive detail has been omitted. In trying to present a book which would be practical and informative, it was found that stress should be placed on basic parts rather than on lengthy discussion of fine details. It was felt that the student would gain more through observing and understanding than through memorizing cumbersome lists of details. As there are several reference books on cat anatomy, it has rather been the aim of this book to present the anatomy of the cat visually.

No attempt has been made to present original research, and the listed reference books have been freely used for their information and terminology.

In this book, only one term for each part has been stressed throughout, with its synonyms listed in the Glossary, since in the field of anatomy standardization of terminology common to both human and comparative anatomy has not yet been achieved. Various international commissions have been appointed in the past to solve the inconsistencies in human anatomical nomenclature. A European commission in Basle, Switzerland, in 1895, compiled a list of terms known as the BNA or B.N.A. for Basle Nomina Anatomica. A British revision adopted in Birmingham in 1933 became known as BR or B.R.; a German revision adopted in 1935 became known as NK or N.K., and a modification of this, published in 1937 in Jena, became known as JNA or J.N.A., and also as INA or I.N.A., since it was approved by a commission established by the International Congress of Anatomists meeting in Milan in 1936. This atlas has favored mostly BNA or BR terms,

and the source of the terms in the Glossary has been designated. OT has been used to indicate old terminology which was derived from American usage prior to the BNA list, while zoological terms not applicable to human structures are listed with no designation.

A Glossary has been included in order to present the synonyms, pronunciations, and derivations of difficult or interesting words. In order to eliminate the necessity of learning a symbol system for pronunciations, the words have been written according to sound, using letters and combinations of letters the sounds of which are common. Thus it should be possible for the student to look at a word and pronounce it correctly. Pronunciations of frequently mispronounced words have been included in the text. The final authority has been *Webster's New International Dictionary* (2d ed., 1948).

HAZEL E. FIELD
MARY E. TAYLOR

PREFACE To Second Edition

The wide use and continued demand for *An Atlas of Cat Anatomy* in the first edition is a tribute to the excellent concept and product of Professor Hazel E. Field and Miss Mary Taylor.

The second edition continues the original purpose of the atlas, and no attempt has been made to change the style. Since the first edition freely utilized B.N.A. terminology, the revision of these terms by the *Nomina Anatomica* was thought to be advisable. In July 1955, the Sixth International Congress of Anatomists met in Paris and approved the *Nomina Anatomica,* now known as *N.A.* or *P.N.A. Revisions* were made and approved at the Seventh and Eighth International Congresses of Anatomists held at New York in 1960 and at Wiesbaden in 1965. Although terminology is constantly being altered, the use of *N.A.* aids the student in learning terms which have functional significance and also helps him to bring his knowledge into closer conformity with recently published textbooks in the anatomical sciences.

In the second edition, terms of direction and orientation have been simplified, and eponyms and synonyms have been eliminated. Revision of some sections, particularly the discussion of the nervous system, has been made in the light of recent literature. Each change in the second edition has been made with the student constantly in mind, seeking to facilitate his successful transition into the other subdivisions of the whole field of anatomy.

BERNARD B. BUTTERWORTH
Associate Professor of Anatomy
University of Missouri

LIST OF PLATES

plate 1   **THE SKELETON**

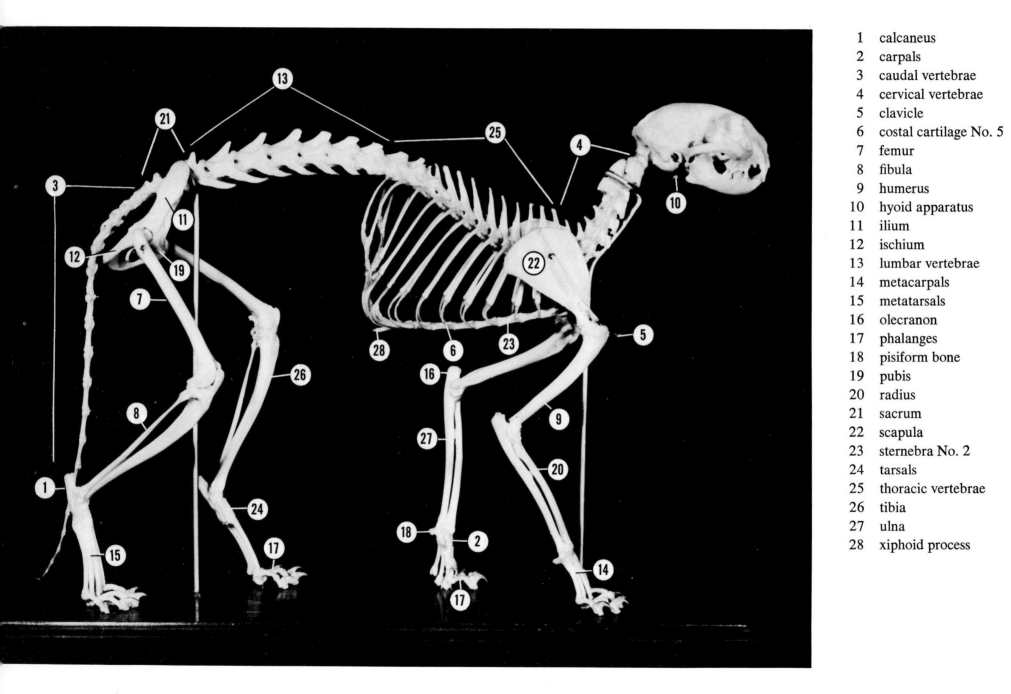

1   calcaneus
2   carpals
3   caudal vertebrae
4   cervical vertebrae
5   clavicle
6   costal cartilage No. 5
7   femur
8   fibula
9   humerus
10   hyoid apparatus
11   ilium
12   ischium
13   lumbar vertebrae
14   metacarpals
15   metatarsals
16   olecranon
17   phalanges
18   pisiform bone
19   pubis
20   radius
21   sacrum
22   scapula
23   sternebra No. 2
24   tarsals
25   thoracic vertebrae
26   tibia
27   ulna
28   xiphoid process

plate 1

SKELETON

of the cat and of most mammals can be divided into the following parts:

I—Axial Skeleton

A—skull

B—vertebral column (spinal column), consisting of

1—**cervical** or neck vertebrae (7)
2—**thoracic** vertebrae, articulating with ribs (13)
3—**lumbar** vertebrae (7)
4—**sacral** vertebrae fused into a sacrum to which the pelvic girdle is attached (3)
5—**caudal** or tail vertebrae (4–26?)

C—ribs (13 pairs)

D—sternum or breastbone, consisting of

1—**manubrium**
2—**sternebrae** (6)
3—**xiphoid process**

II—Appendicular Skeleton

A—pectoral girdle, anterior

1—**scapula,** dorsal
2—**clavicle,** ventral collarbone, vestigial and embedded in muscle in the cat

B—pelvic girdle, posterior, composed of the ossa coxae, each consisting of

1—**ilium,** dorsal, articulating with the sacrum
2—**pubis,** anterior and ventral
3—**ischium** (iss′ kih umm), posterior and ventral

C—limbs; homologies listed from proximal to distal

anterior limb (forelimb)	**posterior limb** (hind limb)
1—**humerus**	1—**femur**
2—**radius,** on side of digit I (thumb)	2—**tibia,** on side of digit I (big toe)
3—**ulna**	3—**fibula**
4—**carpals,** in wrist	4—**tarsals,** in ankle
5—**metacarpals**	5—**metatarsals**
6—**phalanges**	6—**phalanges**

Note that the cat is an example of a digitigrade (dihj′ ih tih grayd) animal, which walks upon its digits and not upon the whole foot, as does man, nor upon the ends of its toes, as does the horse or cow. A **digit** consists of a row of two or three phalanges (fay lann′ jeez) which form a toe or a finger.

plate 2

LUMBAR VERTEBRAE

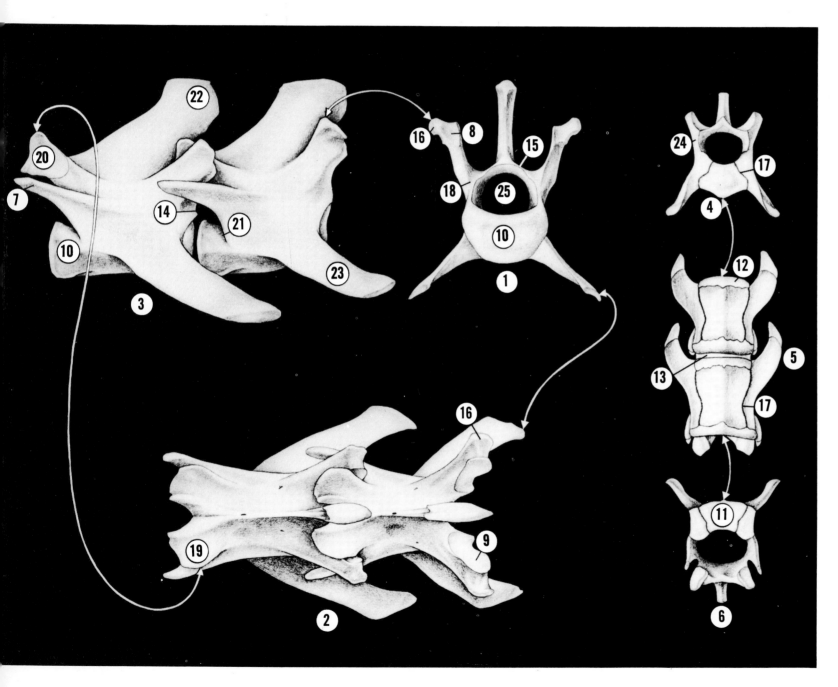

1 third lumbar vertebra, anterior view
2 third and fourth lumbar vertebrae, dorsal view
3 third and fourth lumbar vertebrae, lateral view
4 young third lumbar vertebra with epiphyses removed, anterior view
5 young third and fourth lumbar vertebrae, ventral view
6 young fourth lumbar vertebra with epiphyses removed, posterior view
7 accessory process
8 **anterior articular process**
9 **anterior articular surface**
10 **body**
11 centrum
12 **epiphysis**
13 intervertebral disc
14 **intervertebral foramen**
15 lamina
16 mammillary process
17 neurocentral synchondrosis
18 pedicle
19 **posterior articular process**
20 **posterior articular surface**
21 posterior vertebral notch
22 **spinous process**
23 **transverse process**
24 vertebral arch
25 **vertebral foramen**

plate 2

LUMBAR VERTEBRAE

verr' teh bree. The typical parts are clearly illustrated by the fourth lumbar vertebra. It consists of a large ventral **body** and a dorsal **vertebral** (verr' teh bral) **arch,** in turn composed on each side of a reasonably erect **pedicle** (pedd' ih kehl) and a flattened top, the **lamina,** and surmounted by a sharp **spinous process.** The vertebral arch surrounds the **vertebral foramen** (foh ray' menn), while a series of these vertebral foramina (foh ramm' ih nuh) form the **vertebral canal** through which passes the spinal cord. The articulations of the vertebral column consist of cartilaginous joints between the vertebral bodies, and **synovial** (sih-noh' vih al) **joints** between the vertebral arches. The **intervertebral discs** of fibrocartilage contain the elastic remains of the notochord, which is centrally located in each disc. Note that the posterior articular surface of one vertebra always overlaps the anterior articular surface of the next vertebra like shingles on a roof. Each vertebra possesses a pair of **anterior articular processes** having **anterior articular surfaces,** and a pair of **posterior articular processes** having **posterior articular surfaces.** In lateral view the **vertebral notches** can be seen, which in the lumbar region of the cat are entirely on the caudal end of the vertebra. When the vertebrae are in position, the vertebral notches form the **intervertebral foramina,** through which the spinal nerves pass from the spinal cord. Projecting from the sides of the body of the vertebra and directed ventrally and anteriorly is a pair of conspicuous **transverse processes.** Lumbar vertebrae also possess **mammillary processes,** which are small and found only in the lumbar vertebrae and the seventh to the thirteenth thoracic vertebrae. They received their name from a resemblance in certain human lumbar vertebrae to a nipple or mamma, and they are located at the sides of the anterior articular processes. Directed posteriorly from the pedicle in all the lumbar vertebrae except the last is the small **accessory process.** Both the mammillary process and the accessory process are sometimes considered specialized transverse processes.

DEVELOPMENT

The mammalian vertebra develops as right and left cartilaginous **vertebral arches** and a cartilaginous **centrum** around the **notochord.** These arches join dorsally in a **spinous process** and join the centrum ventrally. The point at which an arch joins the centrum is called a **neurocentral synchondrosis,** which can be observed in young vertebrae and which demonstrates that the pedicle, costal facets, and lumbar transverse processes are formed from the arches rather than from the centrum. After birth, **epiphyses** (eh piff' ih seez) appear at the ends of each central region as small secondary centers of ossification. When maturity is reached, no further elongation of the cartilage takes place, while the bone-forming cells continue their growth, uniting the centrum with its epiphyses to form the **body of the vertebra.** Therefore, the terms **centrum** and **body** are not synonyms, though often so used. In discussions of mammalian vertebrae, the term **centrum** should be used only for the developmental stages.

plate 3   RIB, CERVICAL AND THORACIC VERTEBRAE

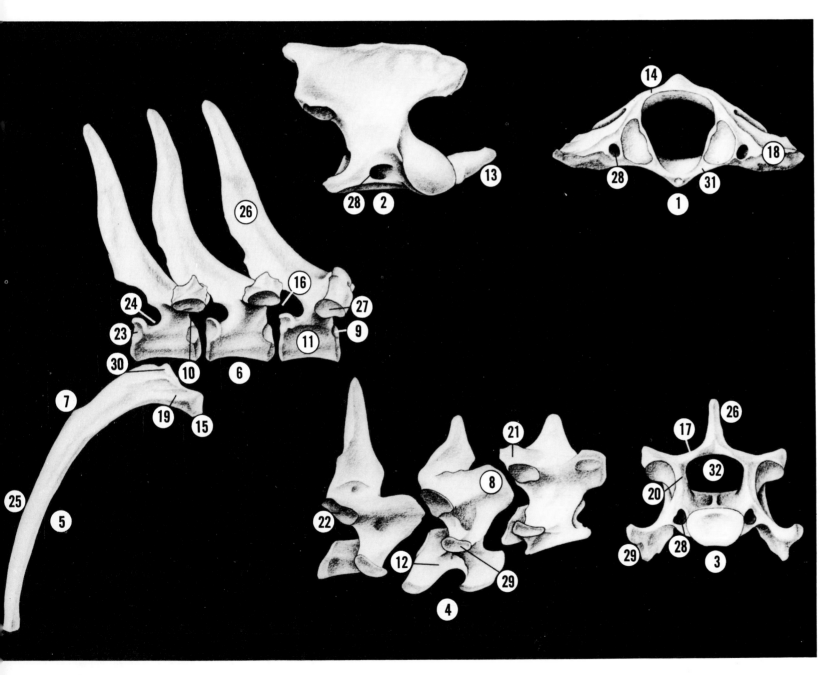

1   **atlas, posterior view**
2   **axis, lateral view**
3   **fourth cervical vertebra, posterior view**
4   **fifth to seventh cervical vertebrae, lateral view**
5   **rib, slightly displaced**
6   **third to fifth thoracic vertebrae, lateral view**
7   angle
8   **anterior articular process**
9   **anterior costal demifacet**
10   **anterior vertebral notch**
11   **body**
12   costal process
13   **dens**
14   dorsal arch
15   head
16   **intervertebral foramen**
17   lamina
18   lateral mass
19   neck
20   pedicle
21   **posterior articular process**
22   **posterior articular surface**
23   **posterior costal demifacet**
24   **posterior vertebral notch**
25   shaft
26   **spinous process**
27   **transverse costal facet**
28   **transverse foramen**
29   transverse process
30   tubercle
31   ventral arch
32   **vertebral foramen**

plate 3

CERVICAL VERTEBRAE

Mammalian cervical vertebrae, in general, possess broad transverse processes, each containing a **transverse foramen,** through which passes the vertebral artery. Each transverse process is composed chiefly of an embryological rib, which has fused to the vertebra, thereby forming the transverse foramen. In the cat the sixth cervical vertebra is peculiar, in that it possesses a sharp projection dorsal to the typical transverse process and transverse foramen. This process is considered to be the transverse process proper, and the other, broader process is called a costal process, from its embryological origin. The costal process shows an anterior enlargement or portion and a posterior portion. A smaller transverse process proper is seen on the fifth cervical vertebra of the cat, in addition to the usual costal process, while the seventh cervical vertebra has an even larger transverse process proper, but no costal process and no transverse foramen.

ATLAS

the first cervical vertebra, so named because the globe of the skull rests upon it in man. Embryologically the centrum (opposite Pl. 2) of the atlas joins the anterior end of the second vertebra, the axis, to form the dens (see below). Because of this loss of part of its centrum to the axis, the atlas has a narrow **ventral arch** in place of the body, while the dorsal portion of the vertebral arch is referred to as a **dorsal arch** and the sides are called **lateral masses.** Lamina and pedicle are indistinguishable. The vertebral foramen is separated in life from the dens of the axis by a short **transverse ligament** extending between two small tubercles. If the transverse ligament is broken, the dens can puncture and tear the spinal cord, and this is often the case when a broken neck results in sudden death. The vertebral artery in the transverse foramen passes dorsally at the anterior end of the atlas through the atlantal foramen to enter the foramen magnum of the skull.

AXIS

second cervical vertebra, so called because it possesses a **dens** around which the atlas turns, producing the rotation of the head from side to side. The dens is formed in the fetus by union of part of the centrum of the atlas with the body of the axis.

THORACIC VERTEBRAE

can be distinguished from all other vertebrae by the presence of **facets** for the articulation of ribs. Typically, the bodies bear **anterior costal demifacets** and **posterior costal demifacets,** which, with the intervening intervertebral disc, make a surface for articulation for the head of a rib between two vertebrae. The transverse processes bear **transverse costal facets,** which articulate with the tubercle of the rib which has its head at the anterior costal demifacet of that same vertebra. Not all thoracic vertebrae are typical, however. The first thoracic vertebra has an anterior costal facet which is complete rather than partial. The eleventh, twelfth, and thirteenth thoracic vertebrae have no transverse costal facets and only one complete costal facet located anteriorly on each side of their bodies.

RIBS

thirteen pairs in the cat, twelve of which have a dorsal bony portion considered the **rib,** and a ventral unossified portion called a **costal cartilage.** The costal cartilages of the first nine ribs articulate with the sternum directly (true ribs), while those of the tenth, eleventh, and twelfth attach to the ninth costal cartilage (false ribs). The thirteenth rib is called both a false rib and a floating rib, since it is completely unattached at the sternal end. The first ten ribs articulate by the **head** with the costal facet or demifacets on the anterior end of the body of the vertebra, and the **tubercle** with the costal facet of the transverse process of the same vertebra. The eleventh to the thirteenth ribs have no tubercles and articulate only by the head to their respective vertebral bodies. The main part of the rib is called the **shaft.**

plate 4

SACRUM, CAUDAL VERTEBRAE, AND STERNUM

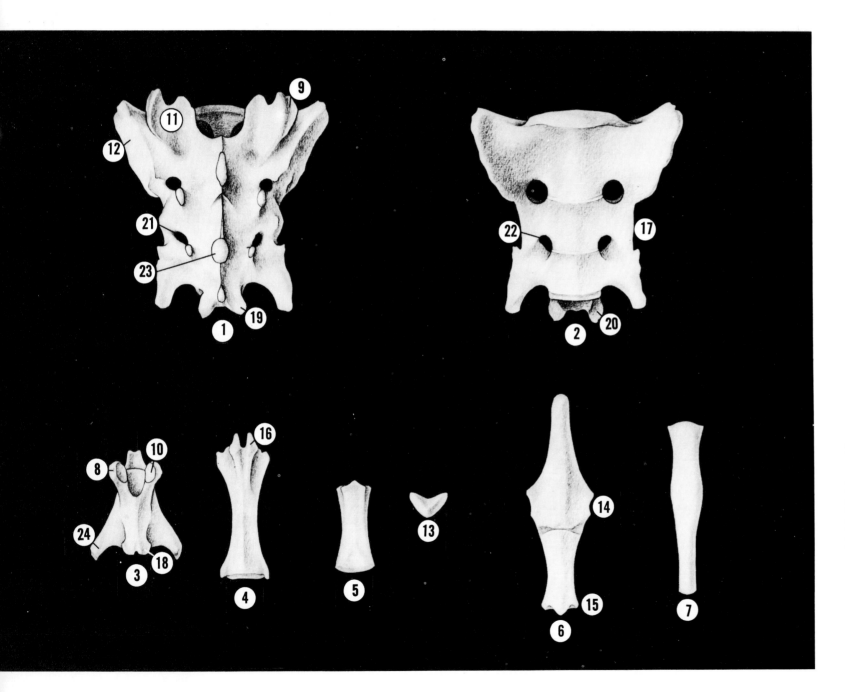

1 **sacrum, dorsal view**
2 **sacrum, ventral view**
3 **fifth caudal vertebra, dorsal view**
4 **tenth caudal vertebra, ventral view**
5 **sternebra, ventral view**
6 **manubrium, ventral view**
7 **xiphoid process, ventral view**
8 anterior articular process
9 anterior articular process of first sacral vertebra
10 anterior articular surface
11 anterior articular surface of first sacral vertebra
12 auricular surface
13 **chevron bone**
14 facet for first costal cartilage
15 facet for second costal cartilage
16 hemal process
17 **lateral mass**
18 posterior articular process
19 posterior articular process of third sacral vertebra
20 posterior articular surface of third sacral vertebra
21 second dorsal sacral foramen
22 second ventral sacral foramen
23 **spinous process**
24 **transverse process**

plate 4

SACRUM

say' krumm—of a cat consists of three vertebrae, two of which are true sacral vertebrae which articulate with the ilia of the pelvis at their **auricular surfaces,** and a third vertebra, which is usually considered a sacral vertebra because it fuses with the other two. It is more correctly, however, a synsacral vertebra derived from the caudal region. Each of the broad, fused, transverse processes on each side of the sacrum is termed a **lateral mass.** Ribs, or costal elements, are included in the transverse processes of the true sacral vertebrae, but it does not seem to be known whether they are present or not in the third sacral vertebra. The fusion of the transverse processes encloses the sacral intervertebral foramina, so that the spinal nerves do not emerge as such from the sacrum but as **dorsal** and **ventral primary di-** **visions** or **rami** through the **dorsal sacral foramina** and the **ventral sacral foramina,** respectively.

CAUDAL VERTEBRAE

show a graded series of diminishing parts. The last vertebra consists of merely a small cylindrical body, while usually only the first seven or eight possess any demonstrable vertebral arch. Their unique character is the presence of tiny **chevron bones,** which enclose the caudal artery and caudal vein and are found near the intervertebral discs at the anterior end of the vertebra. These chevron bones articulate with small ventral processes, the **hemal processes,** also called hypapophyses by some authors. These usually are not preserved in making a skeleton and, in any case, are not to be expected anterior to the second caudal vertebra or posterior to the thirteenth caudal vertebra, although there appears to be great variability in their occurrence.

STERNUM

of the cat can be divided into the **manubrium** (muh niu' brih umm), six **sternebrae,** which compose the body of the sternum, and the **xiphoid process** (ziff' oid), which consists of a pointed, narrow bone and a broader cartilaginous plate, the xiphoid cartilage (Pl. 1). The first costal cartilage is attached to the manubrium; the second articulates at the joint between the manubrium and the first sternebra; the third through the seventh articulate at the joints between the successive sternebrae, and the eighth and ninth articulate at the same joint between the last sternebra and the xiphoid process.

plate 5 SKULL, DORSAL VIEW

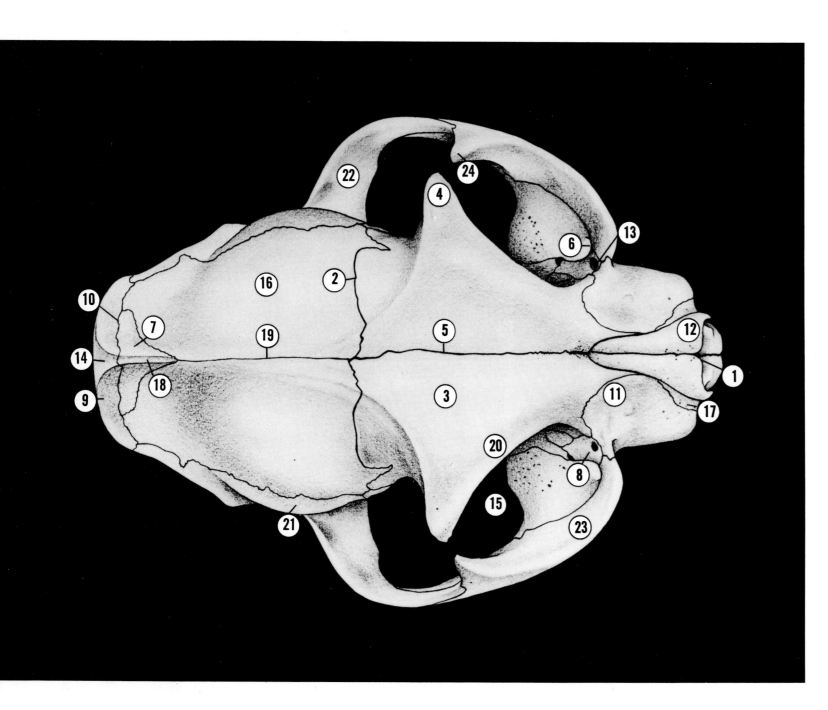

1 anterior nasal aperture
2 coronal suture
3 **frontal bone**
4 frontal bone, zygomatic process
5 frontal suture
6 infraorbital foramen
7 **interparietal bone**
8 lacrimal bone
9 lambdoidal ridge
10 lambdoidal suture
11 maxilla, frontal process
12 **nasal bone**
13 nasolacrimal canal
14 **occipital bone**
15 orbit
16 **parietal bone**
17 **premaxilla,** nasal process
18 sagittal crest
19 sagittal suture
20 supraorbital arch
21 **temporal bone,** squamous portion
22 temporal bone, zygomatic process
23 **zygomatic bone**
24 zygomatic bone, frontal process

plate 5

SKULL

The term skull as used here includes the bones of the face, the jaws, and the cranium or brain case. The hyoid apparatus and the bones of the middle ear are best studied with the skull, whether or not they are technically a part of it. The skull develops from two types of bones: **cartilage bones,** which are first formed in cartilage and are later replaced by bone, and **membrane bones,** which develop directly from a membrane of connective tissue and are never formed in cartilage. In the skull the cartilage bones develop from the embryonic **chondrocranium** (konn droh kray′ nih umm) and **visceral arches.** The chondrocranium in mammals lies primarily under the brain and supports it, while the membrane bones cover the brain and form most of the face and jaws. The bones of the skull develop as follows:

A—from the chondrocranium

1—ethmoid bone, composed of its conchae, perpendicular plate, and lateral masses

2—ventral conchae, articulated to maxillae in nasal cavity

3—presphenoid bone

4—postsphenoid bone, except parts of great wings and pterygoid processes

5—occipital bone, except the most dorsal portion

6—temporal bones, petromastoid portion only

B—from the cartilaginous visceral arches

1—ossicles of middle ears

a—hammer or malleus, from the articular part of the first visceral arch

b—anvil or incus, from the quadrate region of the first arch

c—stirrup or stapes, from the hyomandibular region of the second arch

2—hyoid bone of several ossicles

C—from membrane directly

1—frontal bones

2—interparietal bone

3—lacrimal bones

4—mandible

5—maxillae

6—nasal bones

7—palatine bones

8—parietal bones

9—postsphenoid bone, most of the pterygoid processes, and great wings only

10—premaxillae

11—temporal bones, squamous and tympanic portions only

12—vomer

13—zygomatic bones

ZYGOMATIC ARCH

composed of the zygomatic bone and the zygomatic processes of maxillae and temporal bones. It is said to be a mammalian characteristic, and it bounds the **temporal fossa** posteriorly and the **orbit** for the eye in its anterior portion.

plate 6

SKULL, VENTRAL VIEW

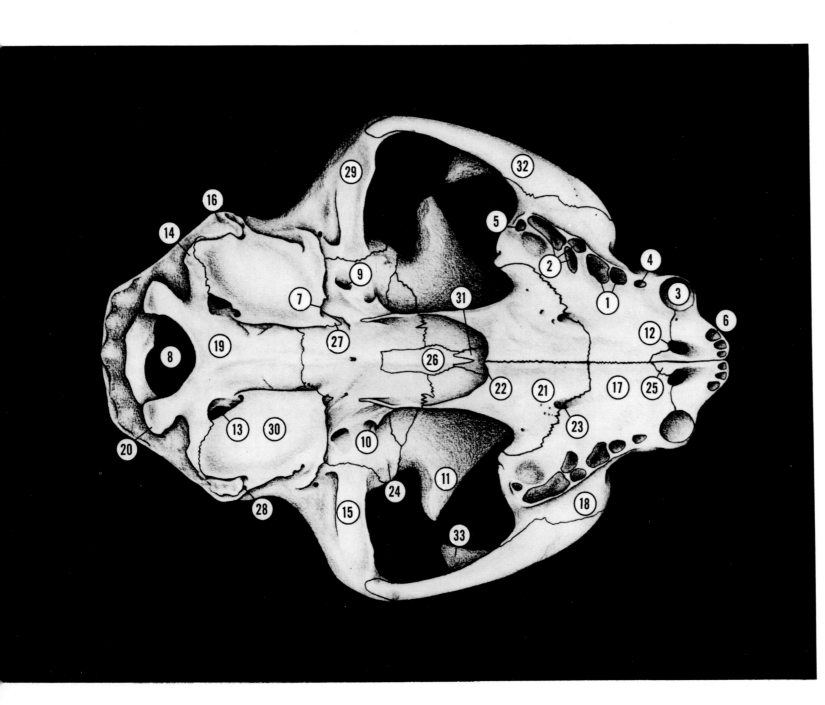

1 alveoli for second premolar tooth
2 alveoli for third premolar tooth
3 alveolus for canine tooth
4 alveolus for first premolar tooth
5 alveolus for molar tooth
6 alveolus for third incisor tooth
7 canal for auditory tube
8 **foramen magnum**
9 foramen ovale
10 foramen rotundum
11 **frontal bone,** zygomatic process
12 incisive foramen
13 jugular foramen
14 jugular process of occipital bone
15 **mandibular fossa**
16 **mastoid process** of temporal bone
17 **maxilla,** palatine process
18 maxilla, zygomatic process
19 **occipital bone**
20 **occipital condyle**
21 **palatine bone**
22 **posterior nasal aperture**
23 posterior palatine canal, anterior end
24 **postsphenoid bone,** great wing
25 **premaxilla,** palatine process
26 **presphenoid bone**
27 styliform process of tympanic bulla
28 stylomastoid foramen
29 **temporal bone,** zygomatic process
30 **tympanic bulla**
31 **vomer**
32 **zygomatic bone**
33 zygomatic bone, frontal process

plate 6

TEMPORAL BONE

three major portions: **1—squamous portion,** thin and flat; **2—petromastoid portion,** consisting of the petrous part, enclosing the inner ear (opposite Pl. 8), and the mastoid part, with air cells and rudimentary mastoid process; **3—tympanic portion,** consisting of an ecto-tympanic part, which forms a ring around the external acoustic meatus, and the entotympanic part, which forms most of the tympanic bulla containing the middle ear. Depending on the condition of the specimen, one or more of the ear ossicles, the malleus, incus, and stapes, may be seen in the tympanic bulla, though usually only the malleus shows plainly.

TEETH

of mammals are set in alveoli or sockets. The incisors, canines, first premolars, and the upper molars of the cat have only one root; the second upper premolars have two roots; and the third upper premolars have three roots (opposite Pl. 7). In the lower jaw the two premolars and the single molar have two roots each. In the cat each root has a separate socket, whereas in man the sockets for each root are usually somewhat united into one alveolus with subdivisions.

plate 7   SKULL, LATERAL VIEW

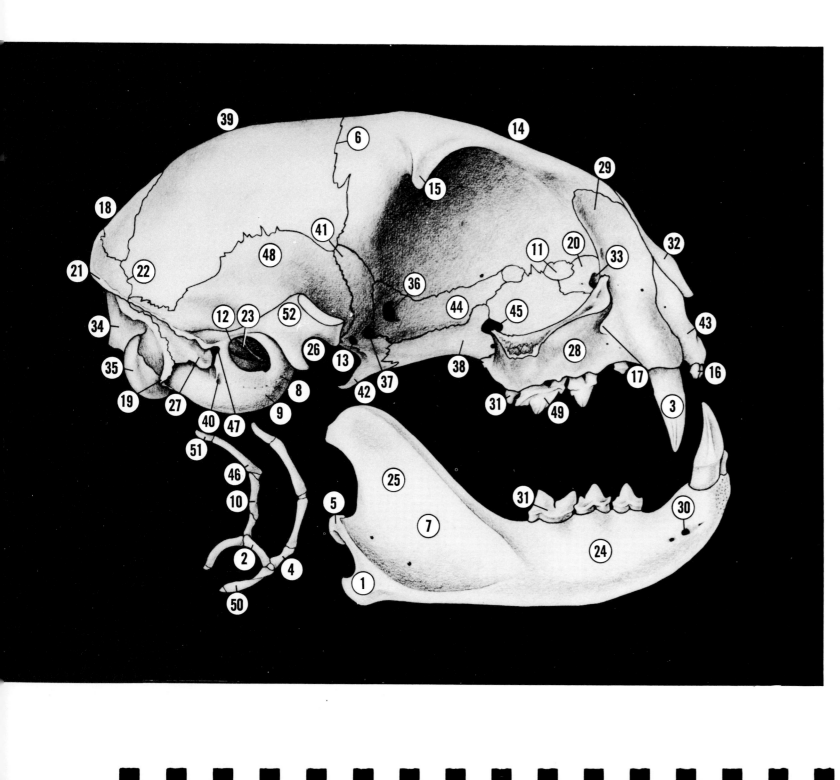

1 angular process
2 basihyal bone
3 canine tooth
4 ceratohyal bone
5 condylar process
6 coronal suture
7 coronoid fossa
8 ectotympanic portion of tympanic bulla
9 entotympanic portion of tympanic bulla
10 epihyal bone
11 **ethmoid bone,** lateral mass
12 **external acoustic meatus**
13 foramen rotundum
14 **frontal bone**
15 frontal bone, zygomatic process
16 incisor
17 infraorbital foramen
18 interparietal bone
19 jugular process of occipital bone
20 **lacrimal bone**
21 lambdoidal ridge
22 lambdoidal suture
23 malleus in middle ear
24 **mandible,** body
25 mandible, ramus
26 mandibular fossa
27 mastoid process of temporal bone
28 **maxilla**
29 maxilla, frontal process
30 mental foramen
31 molar tooth
32 **nasal bone**
33 nasolacrimal canal
34 **occipital bone**
35 occipital condyle
36 optic canal

plate 7 shows the zygomatic bone removed and such parts of the zygomatic processes of the frontal and temporal bones as were necessary to expose parts which would not have been shown otherwise. The hyoid apparatus and lower jaw are shown in their approximate relationship to the rest of the skull.

HYOID APPARATUS

in life connects to the tympanic bulla at a tiny pit just ventral to the stylomastoid foramen. The hyoid apparatus consists of a median element, the basihyal bone, which lies across the margin of the thyroid cartilage and is attached to it by connective tissue. Two pairs of horns project from the basihyal bone. The **anterior horns** consist of a series of four elements, ceratohyal, epihyal, stylohyal, and tympanohyal bones. The tympanohyal bone articulates with the tympanic bulla at a tiny pit just ventral to the stylomastoid foramen. The **posterior horns** consist of one element, the thyrohyal bone, which lies at the side of the larynx (lar' ingks) and is attached to the thyroid cartilage.

TEETH

In the cat there are two sets of teeth: the **deciduous,** or milk, dentition, and the **permanent** dentition. The first set includes six incisors, two canines, and four premolars in the lower jaw, and the upper jaw has the same, plus two additional premolars. The permanent dentition replaces the first set and adds one more molar in each side of each jaw. The definition of a molar varies with the author. The term molar is derived from the Latin *molaris,* a grinder. The human anatomists speak of deciduous molars as those which are replaced by permanent premolars, and of permanent molars as those which are not preceded by any deciduous or temporary teeth. Generally, zoologists write of the permanent teeth, but true molars are never preceded by any deciduous or milk teeth. Size and structure are not included in these definitions.

37 orbital fissure
38 **palatine bone**
39 **parietal bone**
40 pit for tympanohyal portion of hyoid apparatus
41 postsphenoid bone, great wing
42 postsphenoid bone, hamulus of pterygoid process
43 **premaxilla**
44 presphenoid bone
45 sphenopalatine foramen
46 stylohyal bone
47 stylomastoid foramen
48 **temporal bone,** squamous portion
49 third premolar tooth
50 thyrohyal bone
51 tympanohyal bone
52 zygomatic process of temporal bone, cut

plate 8

SKULL, SAGITTAL SECTION WITH NASAL SEPTUM

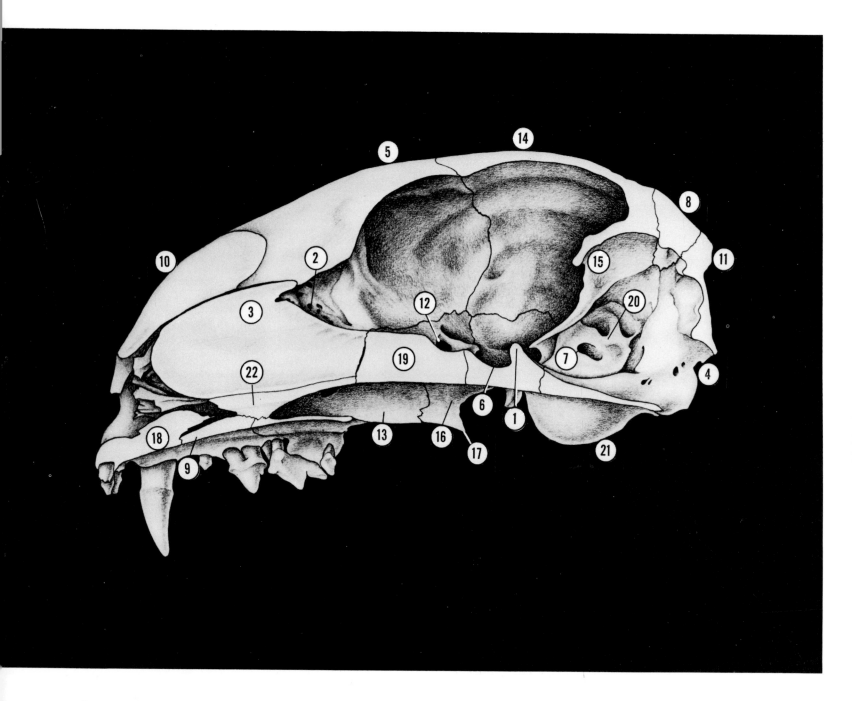

1 dorsum sellae
2 ethmoid bone, cribriform plate
3 **ethmoid bone, perpendicular plate**
4 foramen magnum
5 **frontal bone**
6 **hypophyseal fossa** in sella turcica
7 **internal acoustic meatus**
8 interparietal bone
9 **maxilla,** palatine process
10 **nasal bone**
11 **occipital bone**
12 optic canal
13 **palatine bone**
14 **parietal bone**
15 parietal bone, tentorium
16 **postsphenoid bone**
17 postsphenoid bone, hamulus of pterygoid process
18 **premaxilla,** palatine process
19 **presphenoid bone**
20 **temporal bone, petrous portion**
21 tympanic bulla of temporal bone
22 **vomer**

plate 8

NASAL SEPTUM

The bony part of the nasal septum which divides the right from the left nasal passage consists of the **perpendicular plate** of the **ethmoid bone** above and the small **vomer** below. In life it is completed by cartilage.

INNER EAR

or **membranous labyrinth** is located within the **petrous portion** of the temporal bone, which has been derived from ossification of the cartilaginous auditory capsule (opposite Pl. 6). The membranous labyrinth consists of **utricle, saccule, semicircular canals,** and **duct of the cochlea,** but they are very small in the cat. The **internal acoustic meatus** permits passage of the vestibulocohlear nerve, which includes fibers from the vestibular and spiral ganglia of the labyrinth to the brain.

ETHMOID BONE

a cartilage bone, consisting of a **perpendicular plate,** which comprises the major part of the septum; the **cribriform plate,** through which pass the parts of the olfactory nerve; and the **labyrinth,** which contains air cells and the large mass of the middle concha. In man it also includes the superior concha. A small portion usually can be seen in the medial wall of the orbit.

plate 9

SKULL, SAGITTAL SECTION WITH CONCHAE

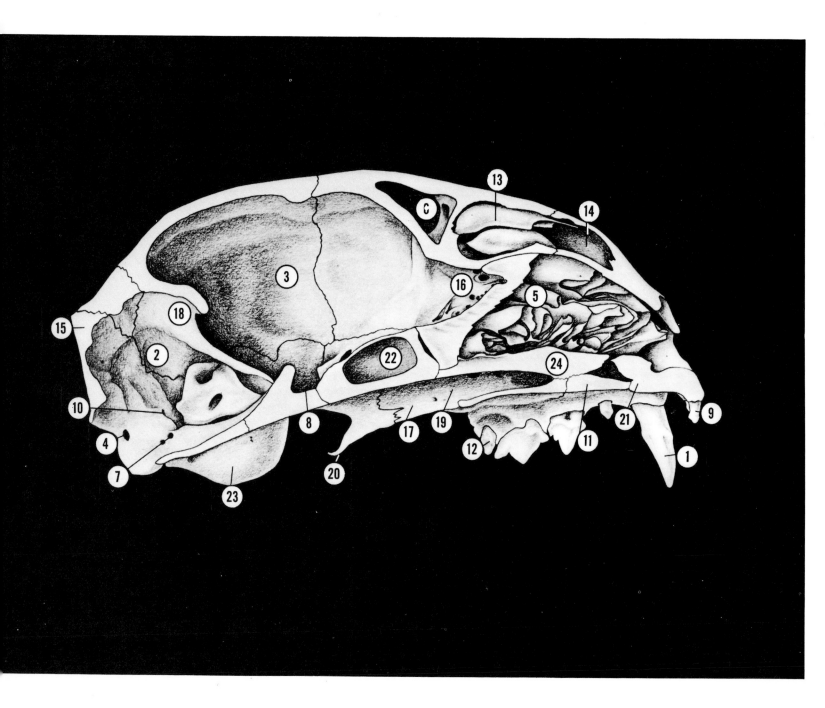

1   canine tooth
2   cerebellar fossa
3   cerebral fossa
4   condyloid canal
5   **ethmoid bone, middle nasal concha**
6   **frontal sinus** in frontal bone
7   hypoglossal canal
8   hypophyseal fossa in sella turcica
9   incisor tooth
10   jugular foramen
11   maxilla, palatine process
12   molar tooth
13   **nasal concha, dorsal**
14   nasal fossa in nasal bone
15   occipital bone
16   olfactory fossa
17   palatine bone
18   parietal bone, tentorium
19   posterior nasal aperture
20   postsphenoid bone, hamulus of ptery-
     goid process
21   premaxilla, palatine process
22   **presphenoidal air cell**
23   tympanic bulla of temporal bone
24   **vomer**

plate 9

CONCHAE

kong' kee—in the cat are not easily divided into three portions, as in man; it is sufficient to note that they are much more folded in the cat than in the human nose, presumably increasing the animal's olfactory sensitivity. In fact, the conchae of the nose of the dog are even more complex. In the cat a small portion, sometimes called the **dorsal nasal concha,** extends into the fossa of the nasal bone. The **ventral nasal concha** (Pl. 11) is a separate bone, only slightly coiled, articulating with the medial side of the maxilla. The main mass is, therefore, to be termed the **ethmoid labyrinth,** or lateral mass, which includes the **middle concha** and the **ethmoidal air cells;** but it may or may not be strictly homologous with the labyrinth and middle conchae of man.

AIR SPACES

The cat skull possesses air spaces called **sinuses** when large and **air cells** when small, in the **frontal, ethmoid, and presphenoid bones.** These are lined with a mucosa which is ciliated in man and presumably so in the cat; they all open into the nose; therefore, they are known as paranasal sinuses in man. There are also said to be **air cells** in the **mastoid part** of the temporal bone of the cat, and they presumably communicate with the middle ear as in man.

CRANIUM

fits snugly around the brain and shows several regions corresponding to regions of the brain (Pl. 55). **1—** The **olfactory fossae** for the olfactory bulbs just poste-rior to the cribriform plate. The olfactory nerves pass from the nasal mucosa on the conchae of the nose to the olfactory bulbs of the brain through the small openings in the cribriform plate. **2—**The **cerebral fossae** for the cerebral hemispheres. **3—**The **cerebellar fossae** for the cerebellar hemispheres, which are separated from the cerebral fossae by the **tentorium** of the **parietal bone.** The tentorium has no bony homologue in the skull of man, though the tough dura mater of man possesses, a fold known as the tentorium cerebelli.

plate 10

POSTSPHENOID, PRESPHENOID, AND VOMER

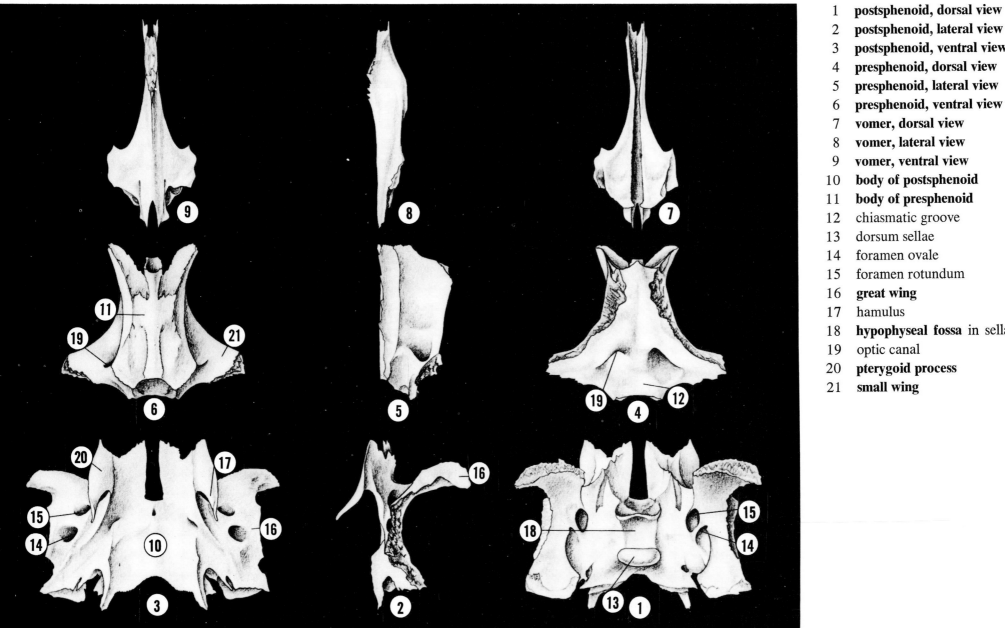

1   **postsphenoid, dorsal view**
2   **postsphenoid, lateral view**
3   **postsphenoid, ventral view**
4   **presphenoid, dorsal view**
5   **presphenoid, lateral view**
6   **presphenoid, ventral view**
7   **vomer, dorsal view**
8   **vomer, lateral view**
9   **vomer, ventral view**
10   **body of postsphenoid**
11   **body of presphenoid**
12   chiasmatic groove
13   dorsum sellae
14   foramen ovale
15   foramen rotundum
16   **great wing**
17   hamulus
18   **hypophyseal fossa** in sella turcica
19   optic canal
20   **pterygoid process**
21   **small wing**

plate 10

shows the postsphenoid, presphenoid, and vomer in the relative positions in which they occur in the skull, though separated here to show the details of each bone. The top row shows the dorsal view, the second row shows a lateral view, while the third row shows the ventral view.

SPHENOID BONES

sfee′ noyd. In the cat there are two bones, the **postsphenoid** and the **presphenoid,** which fuse into one bone, the sphenoid, in the skull of man. The **postsphenoid** consists of a **body,** or basisphenoid, two **great wings,** and the **pterygoid processes,** which help to wall off the nasopharynx. The **presphenoid** consists of a **body,** or presphenoid proper, which contains the **sphenoidal air cells,** and two **small wings.** The **sella turcica** is a saddle-like structure on the anterior or dorsal surface of the basisphenoid; its **hypophyseal fossa** encloses the **hypophysis cerebri** or pituitary body on the ventral surface of the diencephalon of the brain (Pl. 56). Note that the hypophysis cerebri is located centrally in the head and is extremely well protected from injury, from the experimenter, and from the surgeon.

VOMER

chief function is to form a part of the **nasal septum,** which separates the right from the left nasal cavity. The nasal septum consists of the vomer, the perpendicular plate of the ethmoid, and cartilage. The term vomer comes from the Latin, meaning plowshare, because of the resemblance of the human vomer to a plow.

plate 11

PREMAXILLA, MAXILLA, PALATINE BONE, AND MANDIBLE

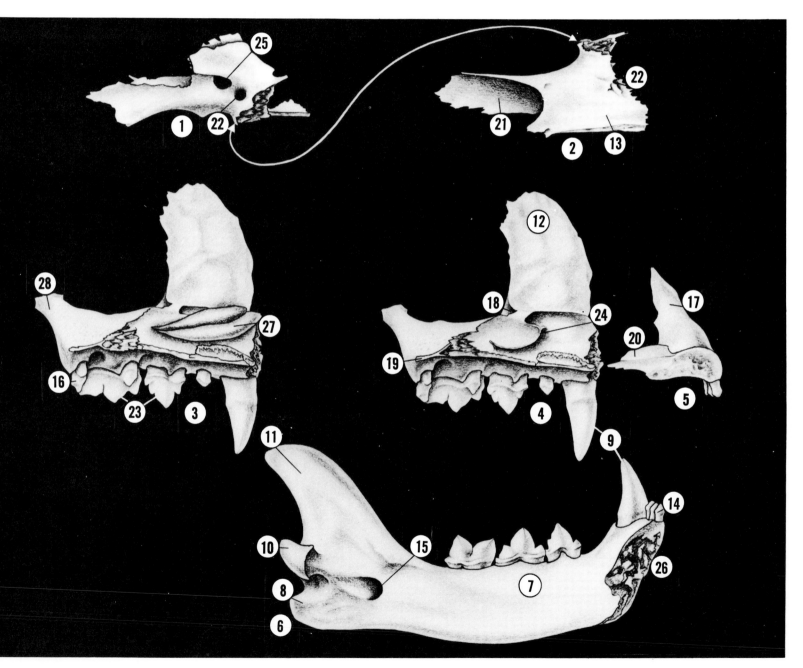

1 **palatine bone, lateral view**
2 **palatine bone, ventral view**
3 **maxilla, medial view with ventral nasal concha**
4 **maxilla, medial view without ventral nasal concha**
5 **premaxilla, medial view**
6 **mandible, medial view**
7 **mandible,** body
8 angular process
9 canine teeth
10 **condyloid process**
11 coronoid process
12 frontal process
13 horizontal portion
14 incisor tooth
15 mandibular foramen
16 molar tooth
17 nasal process
18 nasolacrimal canal
19 palatine process of maxilla
20 palatine process of premaxilla
21 perpendicular portion
22 posterior palatine canal
23 premolar teeth
24 **ridge for attachment of the ventral nasal concha**
25 sphenopalatine foramen
26 symphyseal surface
27 **ventral nasal concha**
28 zygomatic process

plate 11

UPPER JAW

in the cat consists of two separate bones, the **premaxilla** and the **maxilla,** though in man they fuse and are separate only during the growing period. The mammalian **premaxilla** is characterized by having the incisors on its alveolar margin, whereas the **maxilla** has the canines, premolars, and molars. The canine tooth is assumed to be more nearly like the primitive reptilian type than are the other teeth (opposite Pl. 6). The **maxilla** has a **frontal process,** articulating with the frontal bone; an **alveolar process,** bearing teeth; a **palatine process,** separating the mouth cavity from the nasal cavity; and a central **body.** In the cat the body apparently contains no air space, but in man it contains a very large one, the maxillary sinus. It is this maxillary sinus which is separated by only a thin layer of bone from the roots of the teeth of the upper jaw and which can become infected from infected teeth. The ventral nasal concha articulates with the maxilla (opposite Pl. 9).

PALATINE BONE

a curiously shaped bone, which has two main parts, the **horizontal portion** and the **perpendicular portion.** The horizontal portion forms the posterior part of the hard palate at the back of the mouth, articulating with the palatine process of the maxilla. The perpendicular portion helps to complete the nasal cavity and the lower part of the orbit. The horizontal portion contains the larger sphenopalatine canal and the smaller posterior opening of the posterior palatine canal. The posterior palatine canal literally goes through the palatine bone from the small opening in the front of the horizontal portion to a larger opening in the perpendicular portion.

PALATE

consists of the soft palate in the back of the mouth and the hard palate (opposite Pl. 53). This hard palate, which is the firm part of the roof of the mouth, is formed by the palatine parts of the premaxillae, maxillae, and palatine bones (Pl. 6). The palate divides the mouth cavity from the nasal cavity; and, if these bones fail to grow adequately, as in some instances in man, various degrees of cleft palate result.

LOWER JAW

in the cat is easily divisible at the symphysis into a right and left portion, or two dentaries; hence we might conceivably speak of two mandibles, but usage suggests that the cat has only one mandible of two halves. Each dentary bone consists of a **body,** which bears the teeth, and a **ramus,** which projects dorsally for articulation with the mandibular fossa of the temporal bone and for the attachment of the muscles of mastication between the coronoid process and the temporal fossa. The **angle** of the mandible between body and ramus shows in the cat a marked **angular process,** again for the attachment of muscles. The **mandibular foramen** transmits the mandibular branch of the trigeminal nerve, which supplies the mandibular teeth. In man it is used by dentists as the place to inject a temporary pain-killing drug. The term mental as used in mental foramen (Pl. 7) comes from the Latin *mentum,* chin (no connection with the Latin *mens,* mind).

plate 12   PECTORAL GIRDLE AND FORELIMB

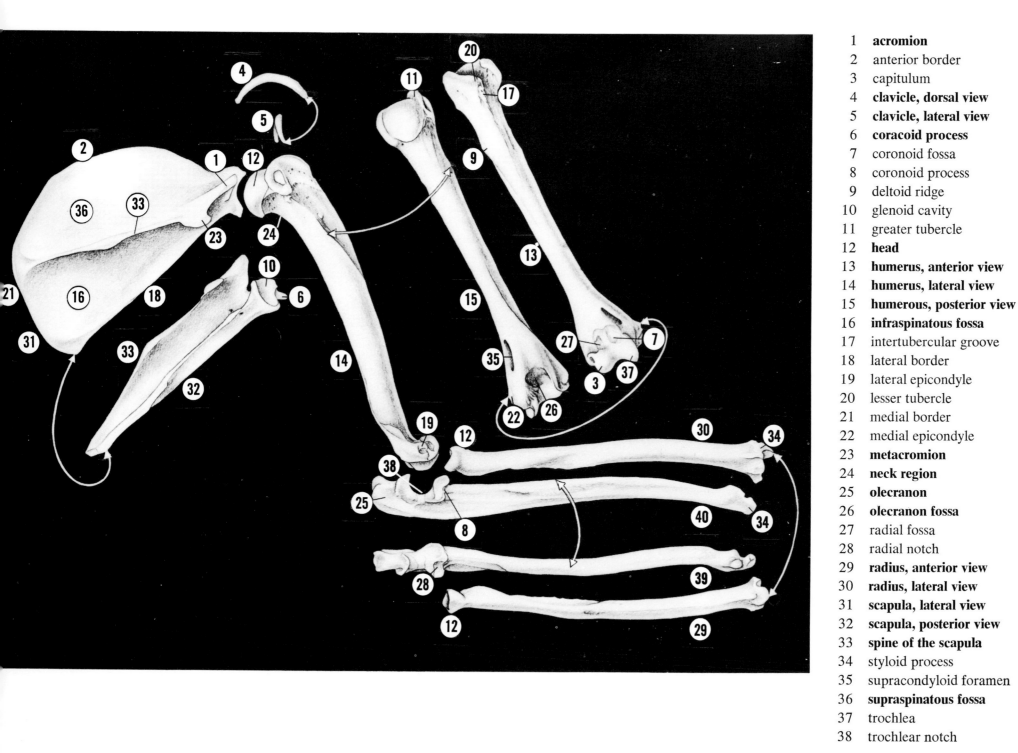

1   **acromion**
2   anterior border
3   capitulum
4   **clavicle, dorsal view**
5   **clavicle, lateral view**
6   **coracoid process**
7   coronoid fossa
8   coronoid process
9   deltoid ridge
10   glenoid cavity
11   greater tubercle
12   **head**
13   **humerus, anterior view**
14   **humerus, lateral view**
15   **humerous, posterior view**
16   **infraspinatous fossa**
17   intertubercular groove
18   lateral border
19   lateral epicondyle
20   lesser tubercle
21   medial border
22   medial epicondyle
23   **metacromion**
24   **neck region**
25   **olecranon**
26   **olecranon fossa**
27   radial fossa
28   radial notch
29   **radius, anterior view**
30   **radius, lateral view**
31   **scapula, lateral view**
32   **scapula, posterior view**
33   **spine of the scapula**
34   styloid process
35   supracondyloid foramen
36   **supraspinatous fossa**
37   trochlea
38   trochlear notch

plate 12

shows the bones of the pectoral girdle and forelimb laterally, in approximately the same position as on the whole-mount skeleton in Plate 1, in order to demonstrate their relationships to one another. Also, as the arrows indicate, additional views are shown of each bone.

PECTORAL GIRDLE

or girdle of the forelimbs is not complete. The **scapula** lies embedded in the muscles and is not in any way attached to the axial skeleton. The **coracoids** are reduced to vestigial **coracoid processes,** useful only for muscle attachment, while the **clavicle** is entirely functionless and is attached to muscle in a raphe (ray′ fee) of connective tissue between the clavobrachialis and clavotrapezius muscles. The clavicle is a membrane bone, whereas the rest of the bones of the girdles and appendages are preformed in cartilage.

DISTINGUISHING CHARACTERISTICS

The **humerus** is easily distinguished from other bones of the cat that are similar in length and general appearance by the shape of its head and the lack of a conspicuous neck, the **ulna** by the olecranon, and the **radius** by its characteristic round head.

HOMOLOGIES

For the homologies between the bones of the pectoral and pelvic girdles and the forelimb and hind limb, see page opposite Plate 1.

PROCESSES

in general are either for muscle attachments or for joint articulations. A **condyle** means a knuckle; therefore, it is always associated with a joint. A **fossa** is a depression or hollow, and a **facet** is any small, smooth surface for articulation.

GROWTH OF BONES

Bones grow either: 1—by enlargement of their surfaces, as does the frontal bone of the skull, or 2—by growing between parts, as in the case of most long bones which form **epiphyses** (development of vertebrae opposite Pl. 2). There are three kinds of epiphyses: **1**—**atavistic epiphyses,** which indicate the probable existence of a separate bone in place of an epiphysis in more primitive animals: **2**—**traction epiphyses,** formed where muscles insert and perhaps even related to sesamoid bones; **3**—**pressure epiphyses,** where bones in use during growth articulate at a joint. When the cartilage cells between an epiphysis and its bone cease to grow, though the bone cells continue to replace the cartilage, the epiphysis becomes indistinguishably fused to the bone. Young specimens show an epiphyseal line where cartilage is still present, or was before the skeleton was cleaned.

39 **ulna, anterior view**

40 **ulna, lateral view**

plate 13   PELVIC GIRDLE AND HIND LIMB

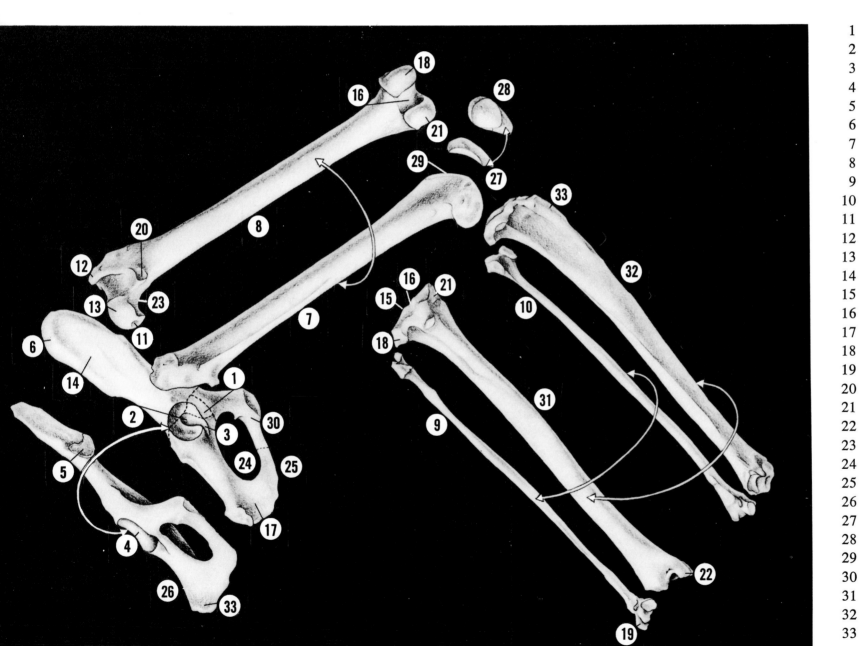

1   acetabular bone
2   acetabular fossa
3   acetabular notch
4   **acetabulum**
5   **auricular surface**
6   crest of ilium
7   **femur, lateral view**
8   **femur, posterior view**
9   **fibula, anterior view**
10 **fibula, lateral view**
11 fovea capitis femoris
12 **greater trochanter**
13 **head**
14 **ilium**
15 intercondylar eminence
16 intercondylar fossa
17 **ischium**
18 lateral condyle
19 lateral malleolus
20 **lesser trochanter**
21 medial condyle
22 medial malleolus
23 **neck**
24 **obturator foramen**
25 **os coxae, lateral view**
26 **os coxae, ventral view**
27 **patella, lateral view**
28 **patella, posterior view**
29 patellar surface
30 **pubis**
31 **tibia, anterior view**
32 **tibia, lateral view**
33 tuberosity

plate 13

PELVIC GIRDLE

or girdle of the hind limbs, is a complete girdle encircling the alimentary canal. Because it is firmly attached to the sacrum, the girdle furnishes strong support for the hind legs. The girdle consists of two dorsal bones, the **ilia,** two anterior ventral bones, the **pubes,** and two posterior ventral bones, the **ischia** (iss' kih uh). The pubes and ischia meet midventrally in an ischiopubic symphysis, and all the girdle bones fuse during growth into a single bone on each side, the **os coxae** (ahs kock' see). In most vertebrates all three girdle bones meet in the **acetabulum** (ass eh tabb' iu lumm), the socket for the head of the femur; but in the cat there is a small **acetabular bone** which actually prevents the pubis from participating in the acetabulum.

PELVIS

Latin word for basin, is the cavity surrounded by the pelvic girdle and the neighboring vertebrae. In man it is sharply divided into a superior false or greater pelvis and an inferior true or lesser pelvis. In the cat it is difficult to see any such division, but the true pelvis is probably that area enclosed by the pubes, the ischia, and the sacral and proximal caudal vertebrae.

ACETABULUM

composed of a smooth, semicircular area, the **lunate surface,** which contains the synovial pocket for the articulation with the head of the femur, and a roughened central region, termed the **acetabular fossa,** for the attachment of the stout **ligamentum teres femoris** (tee' reez), which, in turn, attaches to the head of the femur at its **fovea capitis femoris** and holds the femur in place.

DISTINGUISHING CHARACTERISTICS

The **femur** can be distinguished easily by its round head and distinct neck, the **tibia** by its head with the two condyles, and the **fibula** by its small size. The **distal end** of the fibula is marked by the distinct malleolus (mah lee' oh luss).

plate 14

FOREFOOT AND HIND FOOT

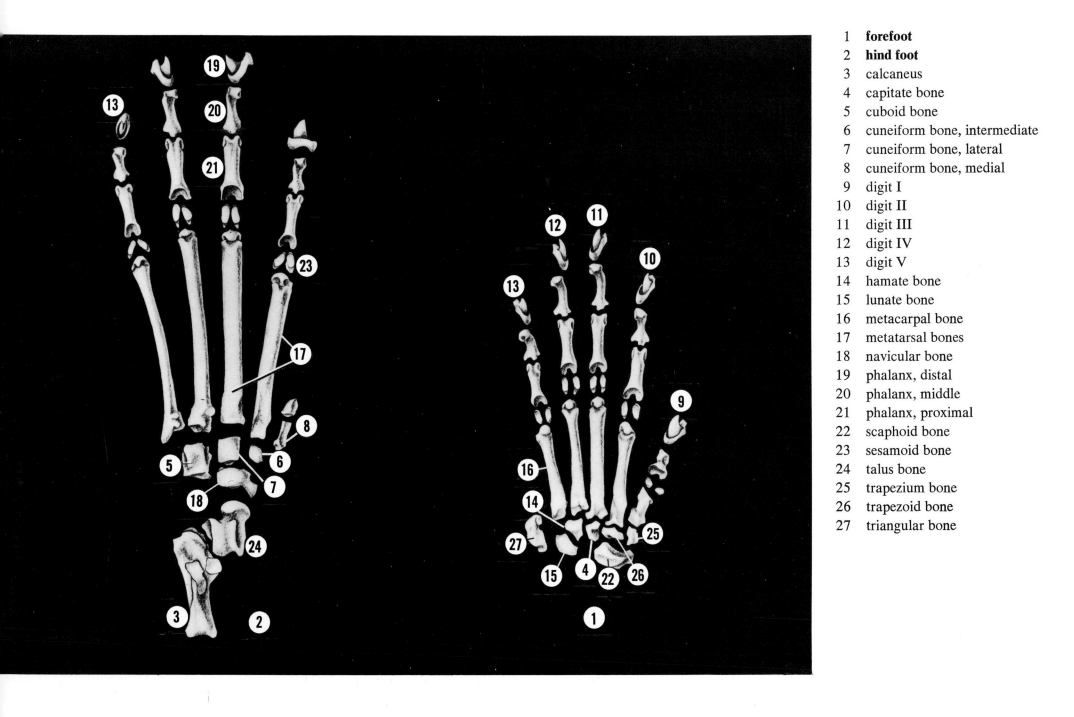

1 **forefoot**
2 **hind foot**
3 calcaneus
4 capitate bone
5 cuboid bone
6 cuneiform bone, intermediate
7 cuneiform bone, lateral
8 cuneiform bone, medial
9 digit I
10 digit II
11 digit III
12 digit IV
13 digit V
14 hamate bone
15 lunate bone
16 metacarpal bone
17 metatarsal bones
18 navicular bone
19 phalanx, distal
20 phalanx, middle
21 phalanx, proximal
22 scaphoid bone
23 sesamoid bone
24 talus bone
25 trapezium bone
26 trapezoid bone
27 triangular bone

plate 14

shows the bones of the forefoot and the hind foot somewhat displaced but in their relative positions to one another. The scapholunar bone is shown here as two bones, the scaphoid and lunate bones, as found in young cats. The pisiform bone has not been shown (Pl. 1). Note that the terminal phalanges are shaped to fit the claws. A claw is a specialized part of the skin and in no way a part of the endoskeleton or bony skeleton.

HOMOLOGIES

In comparative anatomy the **forefoot** or **manus** is considered homologous to the **hind foot** or **pes** and also reasonably homologous to the feet of all vertebrates living on land. The **carpus** or **tarsus** is composed of three rows of **carpal** or **tarsal bones**: 1—the proximal row with three ossicles, including an intermedium in the center; 2—one or more centrales; and 3—the distal row of five **carpales** or carpalia, or five **tarsales** or tarsalia. Homologies of ankle bones of anterior and posterior feet are as follows:

CARPAL BONES OF ANTERIOR FOOT		TARSAL BONES OF POSTERIOR FOOT	
Cat	Comparative Anatomy	Comparative Anatomy	Cat
triangular	ulnare	fibulare	calcaneus
scapholunar	intermedium	intermedium	talus
	radiale	tibiale	
	centrale	centrale	navicular
trapezium	carpale 1	tarsale 1	medial cuneiform
trapezoid	carpale 2	tarsale 2	intermediate cuneiform
capitate	carpale 3	tarsale 3	lateral cuneiform
hamate	carpale 4	tarsale 4	cuboid
	carpale 5	tarsale 5	

SESAMOIDS

are small bones which develop in a tendon. A few become large and receive a special name, such as the patella and the pisiform (pai′ sih form) bone, but most remain very small and have no name other than that of sesamoid bones. Except for the patella and the pisiform bone, most sesamoids are not saved in preparing skeletons. In the cat there are said to be three sesamoids at the knee besides the well-known patella, which develops in the tendon of the quadriceps femoris muscle. The other three are very small and are found in the two heads of the gastrocnemius and the origin of the popliteus muscles. There is also a sesamoid bone in the wrist of the cat, known as a radial sesamoid, in addition to the pisiform bone, two small sesamoids for each metacarpophalangeal joint, and two for each metatarsophalangeal joint.

plate 15

MAMMARY GLANDS

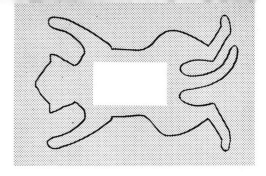

1   great cutaneous muscle
2   **mammary gland**
3   nipple
4   sartorius muscle
5   skin
6   sternal region
7   subcutaneous fascia
8   xiphihumeralis muscle

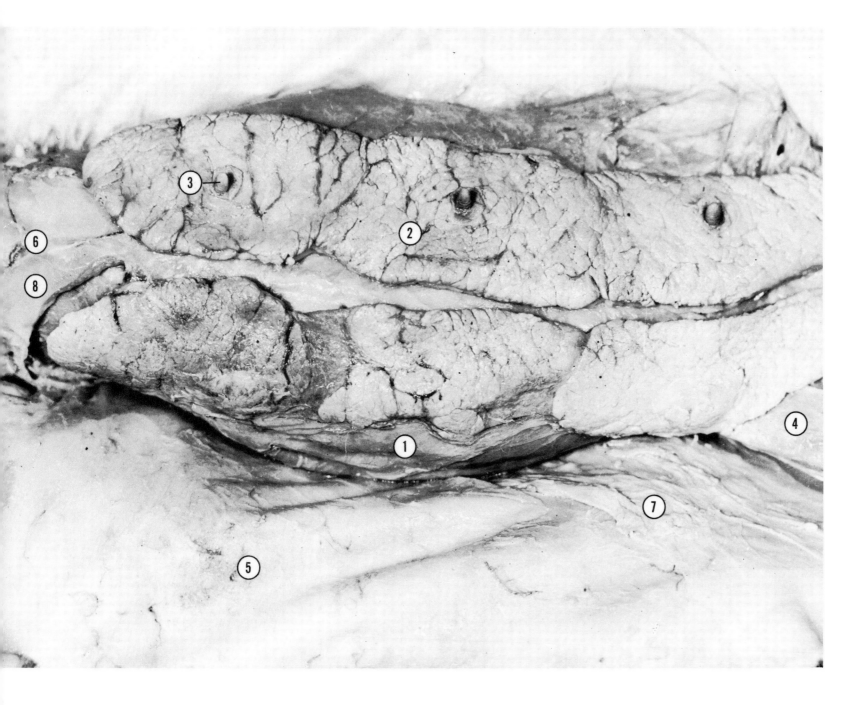

plate 15. shows the skin cut along the midventral line and dissected back, exposing the **mammary glands** of a lactating cat. On the animal's left side the skin has been cut around the three nipples, leaving the nipples in place, while on the other side the nipples have been cut from the gland and removed with the skin.

MAMMARY GLANDS

are found between the skin and the superficial muscles. The bulk of the mammary gland is extremely variable, depending on the state of lactation of the gland, ranging from almost half an inch in thickness in some specimens to a very thin sheet in others. In nonlactating females it is hardly distinguishable from connective-tissue fascia except that it seems more granular in texture and shows more pigmentation. It extends from the groin to the axilla (ack sill' uh) and in some cases overlies the pectoral muscles.

NIPPLES

The normal number of nipples is said to be four or five on each side, and, though the number which actually develop and function is variable, usually at least three on each side are functional. Male cats also have rudimentary nipples, and the mere presence of nipples cannot be used as any guide to the sex of a given specimen.

plate 16   **SUPERFICIAL PECTORAL MUSCLES AND THE GREAT CUTANEOUS MUSCLE**

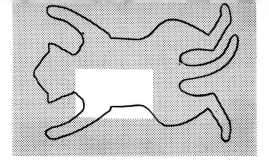

1 clavobrachialis
2 clavotrapezius
3 epitrochlearis
4 **great cutaneous**
5 **pectoantebrachialis**
6 pectoralis major
7 pectoralis minor
8 posterior subscapular nerve
9 sternal region

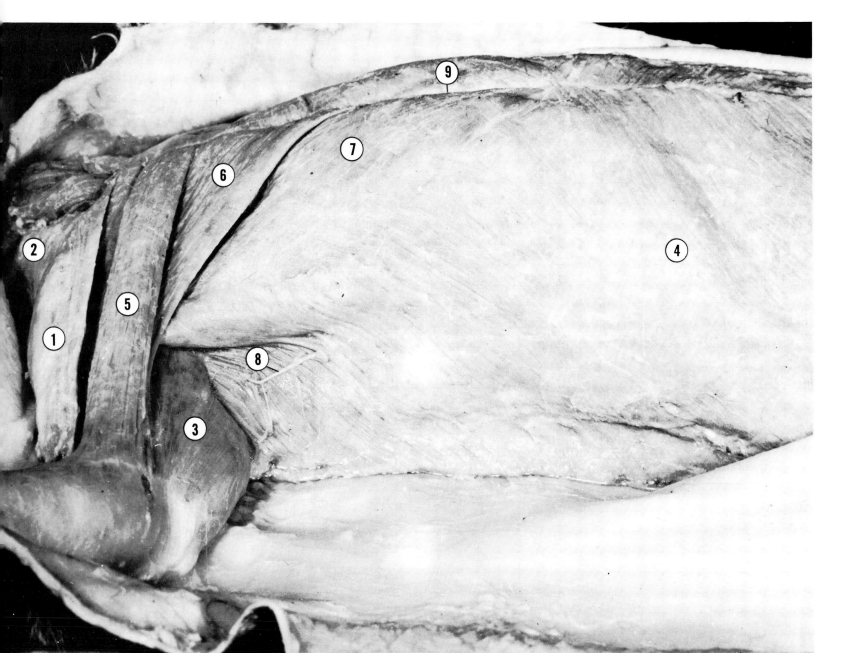

plate 16

shows the skin dissected off the right side of the cat, so that the superficial muscles are exposed.

GREAT CUTANEOUS MUSCLE

Origin: linea alba, and connective tissue and muscles of pectoral region and axilla. **Insertion:** skin in region of middorsal line from shoulder to caudal area. **Action:** moves skin anteriorly and ventrally. See Plate 15, which shows the mammary glands between the skin and the great cutaneous muscle.

MUSCLES: GENERAL CONSIDERATIONS

Voluntary muscles of the trunk and limbs are organs primarily composed of **striated muscle fibers** bound into bundles known as **fasciculi,** which, in turn, are bound into **a muscle** by connective tissue. All muscles, except sphincter muscles, which encircle an opening, have a relatively immovable end, known as the **origin,** and a relatively movable end, known as the **insertion.** These are relative terms. Since all parts of the body are capable of movement, listing origin and insertion is largely a matter of convention among anatomists. For example, the origin and insertion of a muscle may be reversed when one reaches up for an object and pulls it down or when he pulls himself up to the object. When there are two or more points of origin, each is known as a **head** (Lat. *caput*), and the muscle is named according to the number of heads up to four, for example: a **biceps** muscle has two heads, a **triceps** muscle has three, and the **quadriceps** muscle has four. If there are more than four points of origin or if these points are small, they are usually referred to as **slips** or **divisions.** At either end, muscles may **attach directly** to bone or connective-tissue structures, have narrow but heavy connective-tissue ends called **tendons,** or end in flat sheets of connective tissue called **aponeuroses** (app oh niu roh' seez). Tendons and ligaments may look similar when seen in a dissection, but **tendons** are connected at one end to a muscle, whereas **ligaments** connect to bone at both ends or support viscera or similar structures.

In the discussions of muscles for the various plates which follow, no attempt has been made to give all the details of the insertion, origin, and action of the muscles described. Reighard, Jennings, and Elliott give much detail, and the human anatomies give suggestive details for any muscles which are similar to those in man. Muscles may vary slightly from specimen to specimen in their places of origin and insertion, and their action has never been fully studied in the cat. Since even in man, who has been studied long and carefully, agreement has not been reached in many cases about the action of the muscles, we certainly cannot expect to be sure of all the actions in the cat. Consequently, such origins, insertions, and actions as are given are in general terms only.

plate 17   SUPERFICIAL MUSCLES UNDERLYING THE GREAT CUTANEOUS MUSCLE

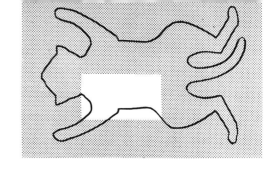

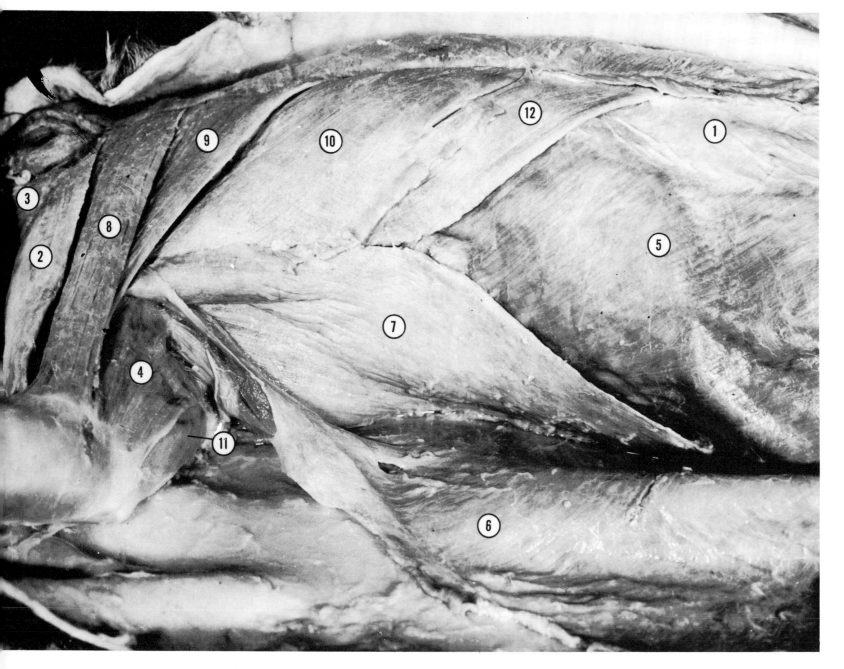

1   aponeurosis of the external abdominal oblique
2   **clavobrachialis**
3   clavotrapezius
4   **epitrochlearis**
5   external abdominal oblique
6   **great cutaneous**
7   latissimus dorsi
8   **pectoantebrachialis**
9   pectoralis major
10 pectoralis minor
11 triceps brachii, long head
12 xiphihumeralis

plate 17

shows the great cutaneous muscle, cut near its points of origin and, except in the axilla, dissected back with the skin exposing the muscles underneath, especially those in the thoracic region.

PECTOANTEBRACHIALIS MUSCLE

peck toh ann teh bray kih ay′ liss. **Origin:** manubrium. **Insertion:** subcutaneous fascia of the antebrachium. **Action:** adducts forearm. It has no homologue in man and derives its name from its insertion as a pectoral muscle on the subcutaneous fascia of the antebrachium.

CLAVOBRACHIALIS MUSCLE

klay voh bray kih ay′ liss. **Origin:** rahpe ventrolateral to, and connected with, the clavicle. **Insertion:** with tendon of brachialis on ulna. **Action:** flexes forearm. The clavobrachialis and the clavotrapezius seem to be continuous, being united by the raphe ventrolateral to, and connected with, the clavicle; they are sometimes named as one muscle, the cephalobrachial or cephalo-humeral.

ACTIONS OF MUSCLES

Muscles are frequently classified according to their principal action. **Flexors** bend a joint, e.g., the biceps brachii bends the arm at the elbow. **Extensors** are the reverse of flexors, e.g., they straighten the arm at the elbow. **Levators** raise a part and **depressors** lower a part, though the term raise is frequently used to mean motion toward the head. The clavotrapezius and levator scapulae are levators of the arm, while the latissimus dorsi is a depressor of the arm. **Adductors** generally move a part toward the median plane or the median axis of either the body or a part of the body, such as the hand, as shown by the adductor femoris or the pectorals, while **abductors** pull the organ away from the median axis, e.g., the gluteus maximus. **Rotators** turn an organ, **supinators** place the hand in the supine position or with the palms facing ventrally, and **pronators** place the hand in the prone position or with the palms facing dorsally. **Sphincters** are circular muscles which make an opening smaller, while **dilators** are muscles which make such an opening larger.

plate 18   PECTORAL MUSCLES, SECOND LAYER

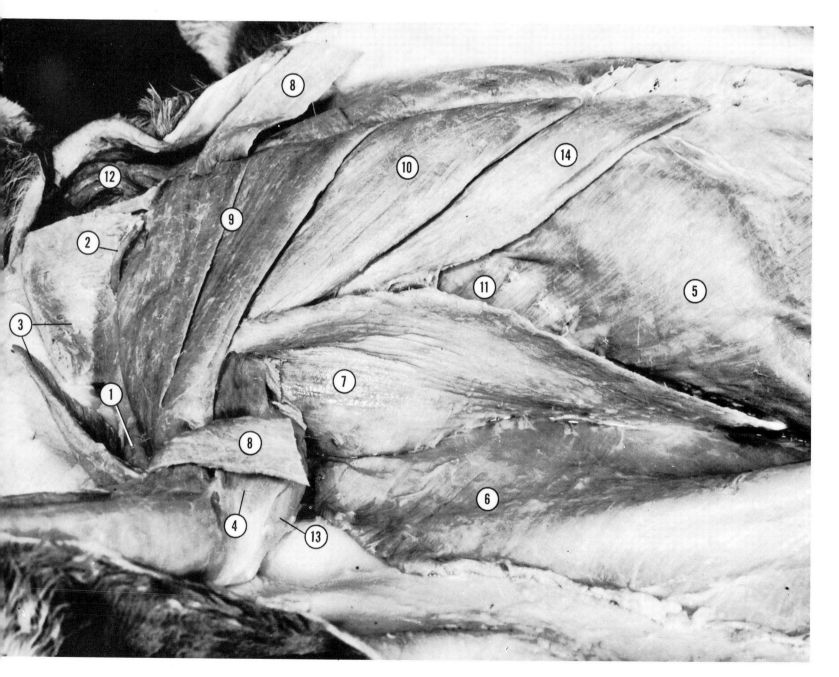

1 **brachialis**
2 clavicle
3 clavobrachialis, cut
4 **epitrochlearis**
5 external abdominal oblique
6 great cutaneous
7 **latissimus dorsi**
8 pectoantebrachialis, cut
9 **pectoralis major**
10 **pectoralis minor**
11 serratus ventralis
12 sternomastoid
13 triceps brachii, long head
14 **xiphihumeralis**

plate 18 shows the clavobrachialis and pectoantebrachialis bisected and laid back to expose the underlying pectoral muscles, from which most of the connective tissue has been dissected.

PECTORALIS MAJOR MUSCLE

peck toh ray′ liss—often found divided into two portions, a superficial portion originating on the manubrium of the sternum, and a deep portion originating on the anterior sternebrae, with both inserting along the crest of the greater tubercle of the humerus. This muscle varies greatly, sometimes showing as many as three or even four parts. They are all considered parts of one muscle because of this variability in different individuals and because they have practically the same origin, the same insertion, and nearly parallel fasciculi. **Origin:** raphe of the median plane and underlying sternum. **Insertion:** humerus between the biceps brachii and the brachialis. In addition, some fasciculi often insert distally with the insertion of the epitrochlearis and pectoantebrachialis. **Action:** adducts the arm and may help in numerous other functions. Those suggested have been: to rotate the arm, to draw the arm posteriorly, to draw the arm anteriorly, and to aid in expanding the chest. This illustrates how difficult it is to determine all the actions of any given muscle.

EPITROCHLEARIS MUSCLE

epp ih trock lee ay′ riss—a thin, flat muscle with no normal homologue in man, though a similar muscle may occur as a variation. **Origin:** latissimus dorsi in the axilla near one point of origin of the great cutaneous. **Insertion:** with pectoantebrachialis on olecranon of ulna. **Action:** assumed to extend the arm.

plate 19

PECTORALIS MINOR AND LATISSIMUS DORSI MUSCLES

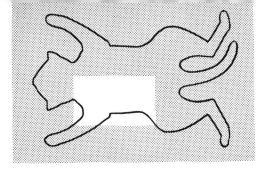

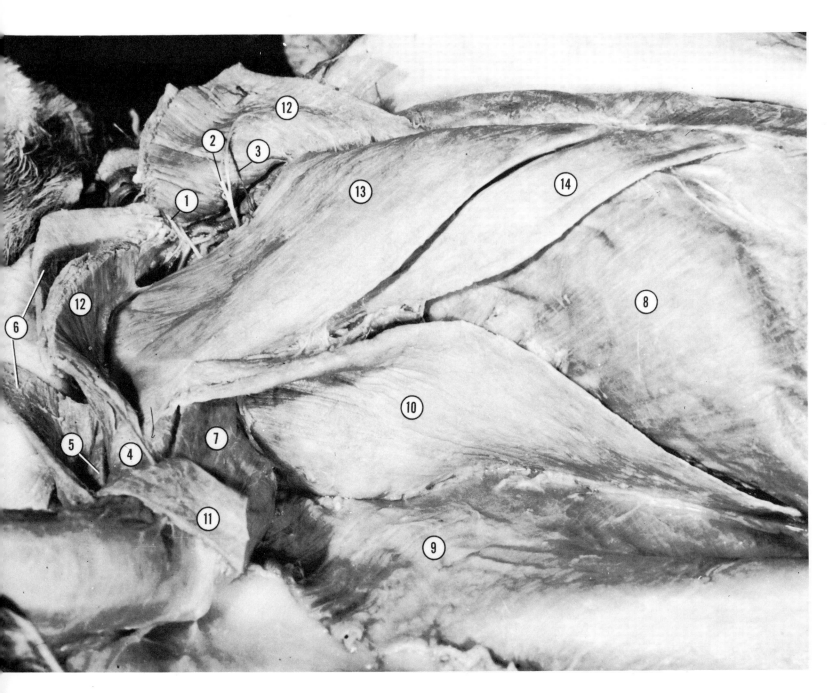

1   anterior thoracic artery
2   anterior thoracic nerve
3   anterior thoracic vein
4   **biceps brachii**
5   **brachialis**
6   clavobrachialis, cut
7   epitrochlearis
8   external abdominal oblique
9   great cutaneous
10   **latissimus dorsi**
11   pectoantebrachialis, cut
12   pectoralis major, cut
13   **pectoralis minor**
14   **xiphihumeralis**

plate 19

shows the pectoralis major muscle bisected, with the ends laid back to expose the pectoralis minor.

PECTORALIS MINOR MUSCLE

Origin: sternum. **Insertion:** humerus just medial to, or underneath, the insertion of the pectoralis major. Both insert between the brachialis and biceps brachii muscles. **Action:** adducts arm; is also said to rotate the arm, draw scapula posteriorly, and move the ribs anteriorly. It is larger than the pectoralis major in the cat, but both are homologous to the human muscles of the same name, and in man the pectoralis minor is relatively small. Note the difference in direction of the fasciculi of the pectoralis major and the pectoralis minor muscles. The pectoralis minor of the cat frequently seems to be divided into an anterior portion and a posterior portion.

BICEPS BRACHII MUSCLE

bai′ sepps bray′ kih ai. **Origin:** scapula. **Insertion:** tuberosity of the radius. **Action:** flexes arm. The biceps brachii of man has two heads, but in the cat there is only one head, which is probably homologous to the long head of the biceps brachii in man.

BRACHIALIS MUSCLE

bray kih ay′ liss. **Origin:** lateral surface of the humerus, partially underneath the acromiodeltoid muscle (Pl. 23). **Insertion:** ulna, again partially covered by the brachioradialis. **Action:** flexes arm.

LATISSIMUS DORSI MUSCLE

luh tiss′ ih muss dor′ sai—the broadest muscle of the back. **Origin:** middorsal line. **Insertion:** humerus. **Action:** extends, adducts and rotates arm medially. It is especially useful to the cat in climbing.

plate 20

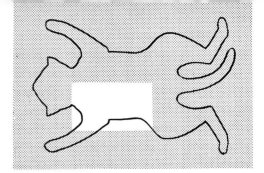

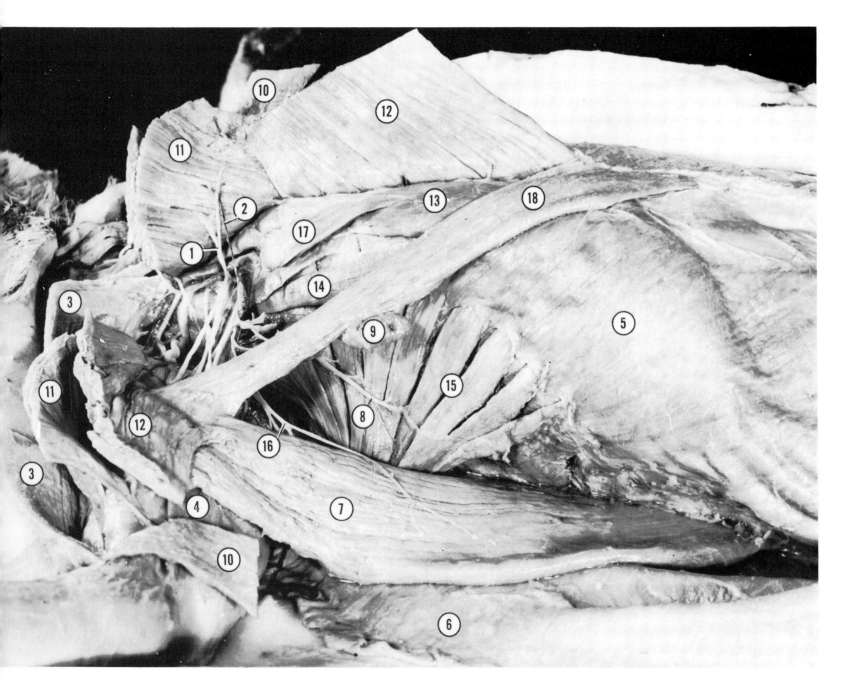

1 anterior thoracic nerve
2 anterior thoracic vein
3 clavobrachialis, cut
4 epitrochlearis
5 external abdominal oblique
6 great cutaneous
7 **latissimus dorsi**
8 long thoracic nerve
9 lymph node
10 pectoantebrachialis, cut
11 pectoralis major, cut
12 pectoralis minor, cut
13 rectus abdominis
14 scalenus medius
15 serratus ventralis
16 thoracodorsal nerve
17 **transversus costarum**
18 **xiphihumeralis**

plate 20

shows all the pectoral muscles, except the slender xiphihumeralis, cut and reflected, revealing the deeper thoracic muscles, the brachial plexus, and the blood vessels of the axilla. The brachial plexus is a group of branching and uniting nerves found in the axilla. It is derived from the fifth, sixth, seventh, and eighth cervical and first thoracic nerves and supplies the foreleg, shoulder, and adjacent areas (Pl. 54). A nerve plexus does not imply any uniting of nerve fibers but only a regrouping, with each fiber retaining its original identity at all times. Arteries and veins are also present in this region and usually are all well embedded in fat.

XIPHIHUMERALIS MUSCLE

ziff ih hiu merr ay' liss. **Origin:** xiphoid process of the sternum. **Insertion:** by a long thin tendon on the humerus deep to the insertion of the pectoralis minor. **Action:** assumed to draw the arm posteriorly and medially. It has no homologue in man.

TRANSVERSUS COSTARUM MUSCLE

Origin: sternum. **Insertion:** first rib and costal cartilage. **Action:** assumed to draw sternum anteriorly. It is a small, thin muscle with no homologue in man, which overlies the thin tendon of the anterior end of the rectus abdominis muscle and is easily confused with it.

plate 21   MUSCLES OF AXILLARY REGION

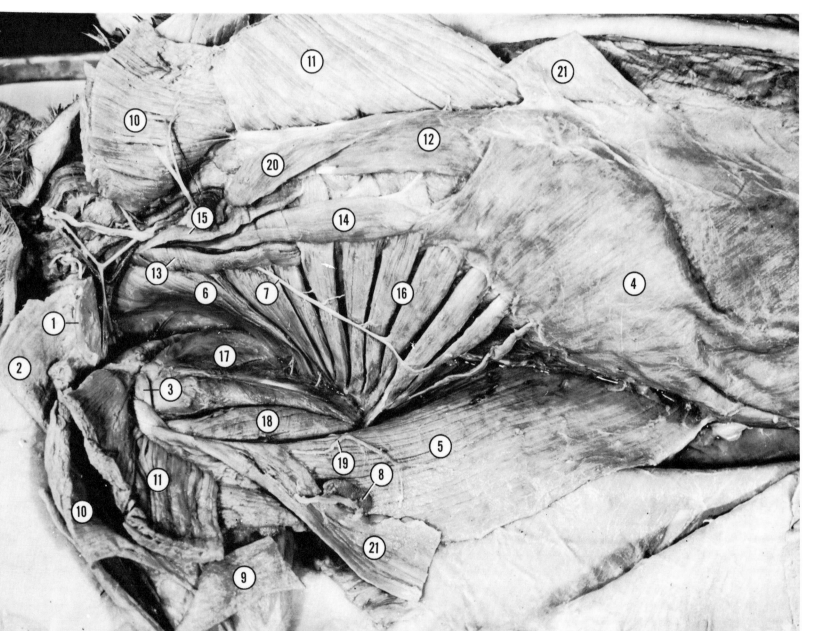

1   **clavicle**
2   clavobrachialis, cut
3   **coracobrachialis**
4   external abdominal oblique
5   latissimus dorsi
6   **levator scapulae**
7   **long thoracic nerve**
8   lymph node
9   pectoantebrachialis, cut
10 pectoralis major, cut
11 pectoralis minor, cut
12 rectus abdominis
13 **scalenus dorsalis**
14 **scalenus medius**
15 **scalenus ventralis**
16 **serratus ventralis**
17 **subscapularis**
18 **teres major**
19 thoracodorsal nerve
20 transversus costarum
21 xiphihumeralis, cut

plate 21

shows all the pectoral muscles cut and most of the brachial plexus of nerves and the axillary artery and vein with their large branches removed. This exposes the underlying muscles on the thoracic wall and those on the medial side of the scapula.

SCALENUS MUSCLES

skay lee' nuss—a complex muscle only partly visible without considerable dissection of the neck. **Origin:** There are three main parts: **1**—The **scalenus dorsalis,** with origin on the third and fourth ribs. **2**—The **scalenus medius,** larger, with origin usually on the sixth to the ninth ribs by thin tendons (Pl. 27). **3**—The **scalenus ventralis,** with origin usually on the second and third ribs. **Insertion:** transverse processes of the cervical vertebrae. **Action:** flexes the neck or draws ribs anteriorly. The scalenus muscles illustrate the difficulty in determining which end of a muscle is the more movable end. Some authorities on human anatomy state that the scalenus has its origin from the vertebrae and its insertion on the ribs.

SERRATUS VENTRALIS MUSCLE

Origin: a series of slips from the first nine or ten ribs, and it is this series of heads that gives it the toothed or serrated appearance which led to its name. **Insertion:** scapula. **Action:** pulls scapula ventrally and posteriorly.

LEVATOR SCAPULAE MUSCLE

leh vay' terr skapp' iu lee—continuous with the serratus ventralis at its anterior border—in fact, so much so that it is sometimes considered a part of the serratus ventralis. **Origin:** transverse processes of cervical vertebrae. **Insertion:** scapula. **Action:** draws scapula ventrally and anteriorly.

SUBSCAPULARIS MUSCLE

subb skapp iu lay' riss—a large flat muscle occupying almost the entire subscapular fossa. **Origin:** surface of the subscapular fossa and also from long strips of connective tissue called laminae, which intersect the muscle and are in turn attached to the scapula. This produces the effect of several slips. **Insertion:** by a strong tendon to the lesser tubercle of the humerous. **Action:** adducts the arm.

TERES MAJOR MUSCLE

tee' reez—parallel to the posterior border of the scapula. **Origin:** vertebral part of the posterior border of the scapula and adjoining fascia. **Insertion:** humerus by a tendon common with that of the latissimus dorsi. **Action:** rotates and flexes humerus.

plate 22

MUSCLES OF FORELIMB, MEDIAL VIEW

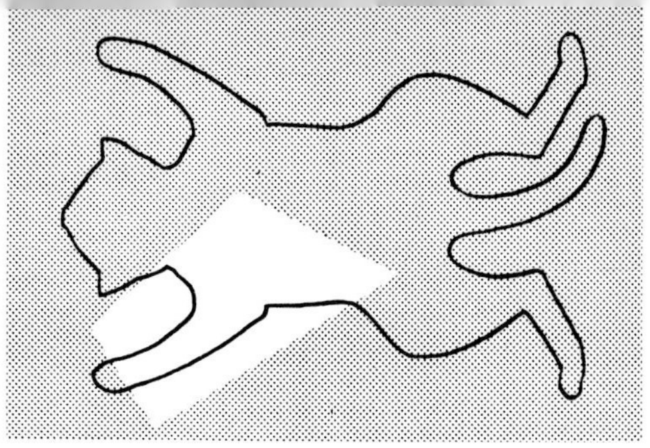

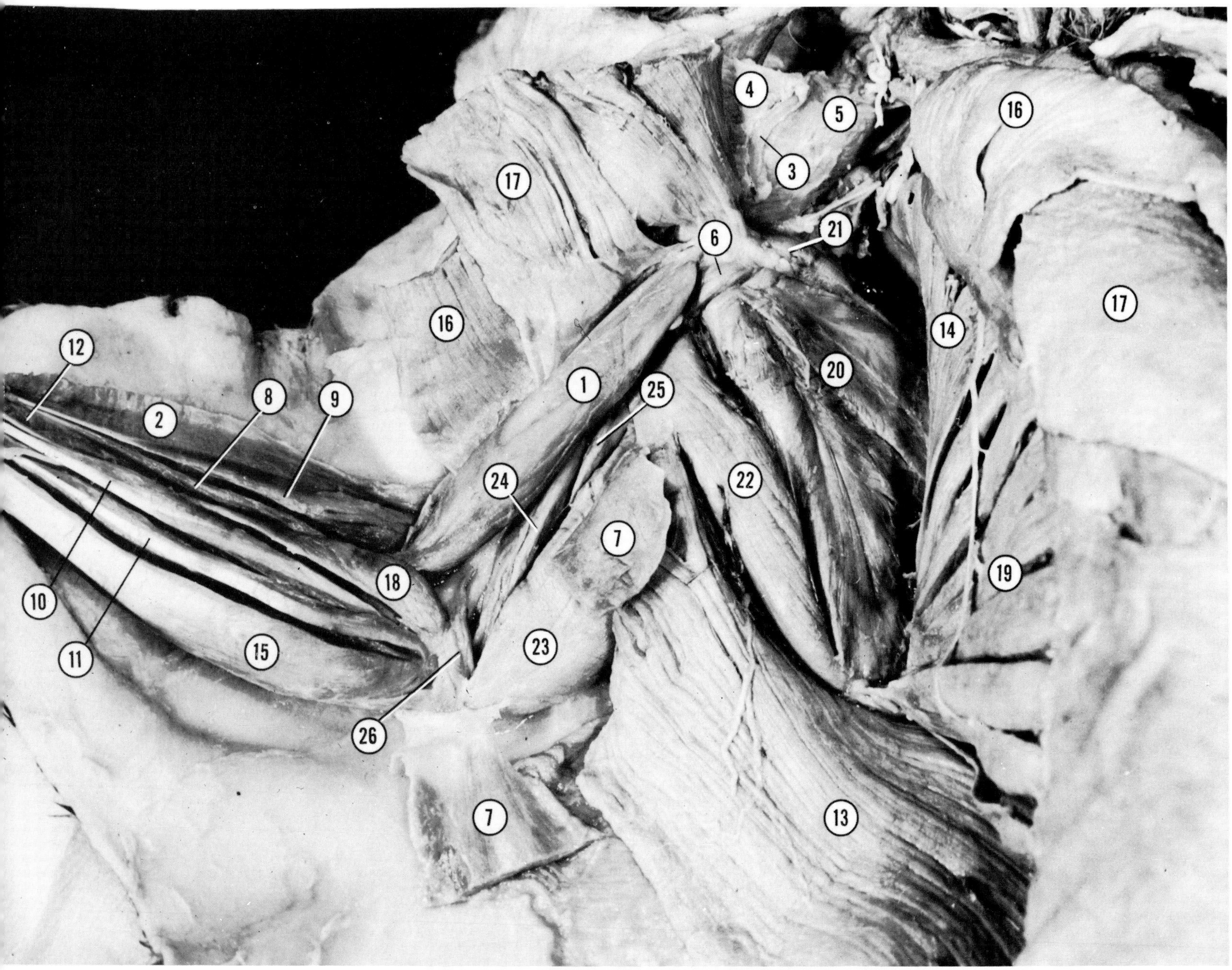

1   **biceps brachii**
2   brachioradialis
3   **clavicle**
4   clavobrachialis, cut
5   clavotrapezius
6   **coracobrachialis**
7   epitrochlearis, cut
8   **extensor carpi radialis brevis**
9   **extensor carpi radialis longus**
10 **flexor carpi radialis**
11 **flexor digitorum profundus, third head**
12 **flexor digitorum profundus, fifth head**
13 latissimus dorsi
14 levator scapulae
15 palmaris longus
16 pectoralis major, cut
17 pectoralis minor, cut
18 **pronator teres**
19 serratus ventralis
20 subscapularis
21 supraspinatus
22 teres major
23 triceps brachii, long head
24 **triceps brachii, medial head, intermediate portion**
25 **triceps brachii, medial head, long portion**
26 **triceps brachii, medial head, short portion**

plate 22 shows the right forelimb laid back from the body, exposing the muscles on the medial side of the shoulder and arm. The epitrochlearis has been cut to demonstrate the medial head of the triceps brachii, which has been separated into its three parts.

TRICEPS BRACHII MUSCLE

medial head. **Origin:** long, intermediate, and short portions on humerus. **Insertion:** olecranon. **Action:** extends forearm (opposite Pl. 23).

CORACOBRACHIALIS MUSCLE

kor' uh koh bray kih ay' liss. **Origin:** coracoid process of scapula. **Insertion:** proximal end of humerus. **Action:** adducts humerus. In some cats it has a part which inserts on the humerus near the middle of the bone, as the entire muscle does in man.

PALMARIS LONGUS MUSCLE

pal may' riss. **Origin:** medial epicondyle of humerus. **Insertion:** proximal phalanx of each digit and pad of foot. **Action:** flexes proximal phalanx of each digit.

FLEXOR CARPI RADIALIS MUSCLE

karr' pai ray dih ay' liss. **Origin:** medial epicondyle of humerus. **Insertion:** bases of second and third metacarpals. **Action:** flexes hand.

FLEXOR DIGITORUM PROFUNDUS MUSCLE

dihj ih toh' rumm. **Origin:** five heads—three from the medial epicondyle of the humerus, one from the radius, one from the ulna. **Insertion:** bases of distal phalanges. **Action:** flexes all the digits.

PRONATOR TERES MUSCLE

pro nay' tor tee' reez. **Origin:** medial epicondyle of humerus. **Insertion:** medial border of radius. **Action:** pronates hand.

EXTENSOR CARPI RADIALIS BREVIS MUSCLE

bree' viss. **Origin:** lateral supracondylar ridge of humerus. **Insertion:** third metacarpal. **Action:** extends forefoot.

EXTENSOR CARPI RADIALIS LONGUS MUSCLE

Origin: lateral supracondylar ridge of humerus. **Insertion:** second metacarpal. **Action:** extends forefoot.

BRACHIORADIALIS MUSCLE

bray' kih oh ray dih ay' liss. **Origin:** shaft of humerus near middle. **Insertion:** styloid process of radius. **Action:** flexes forearm.

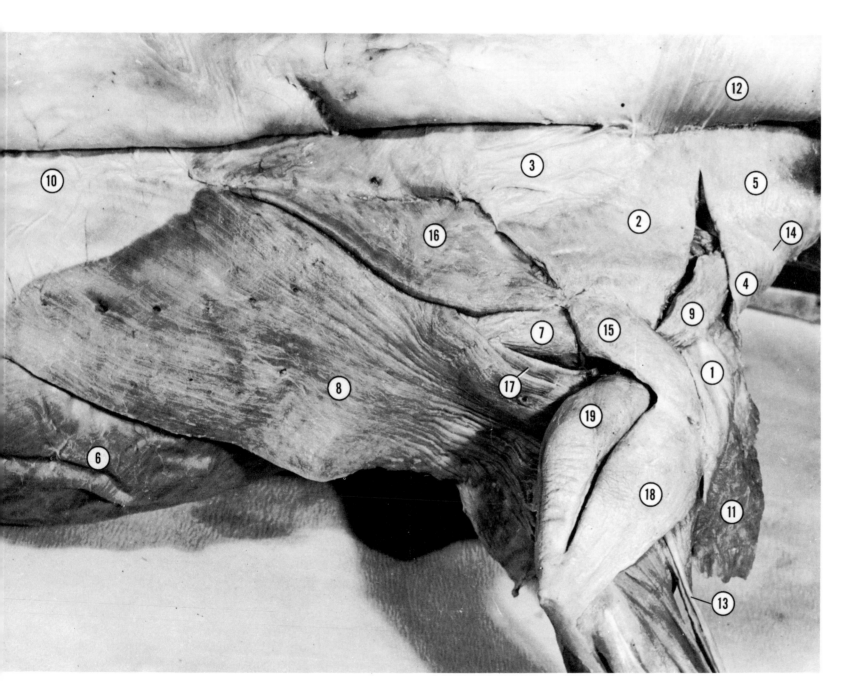

1 **acromiodeltoideus**
2 **acromiotrapezius**
3 **aponeurosis between right and left ac-romiotrapezii**
4 clavobrachialis
5 **clavotrapezius**
6 external abdominal oblique
7 infraspinatus
8 latissimus dorsi
9 levator scapulae ventralis
10 **lumbar aponeurosis**
11 pectoralis major, cut
12 **platysma**
13 radial nerve, superficial branch
14 **raphe between clavobrachialis and clavotrapezius**
15 **spinodeltoideus**
16 **spinotrapezius**
17 teres major
18 **triceps brachii, lateral head**
19 **triceps brachii, long head**

plate 23

shows the skin dissected off beyond the middorsal line, exposing the muscles of the shoulder underneath and the platysma muscle on the skin.

PLATYSMA MUSCLE

pluh tizz' muh. **Origin:** skin and its fasciae near the middorsal line from the skull to the first thoracic vertebra. **Insertion:** skin and various structures around the eyes and mouth. **Action:** moves skin of neck and face.

TRAPEZIUS MUSCLE

truh pee' zih uss—represented in the cat by three muscles: **clavotrapezius, acromiotrapezius, spinotrapezius.** 1—**Clavotrapezius** (klay' voh truh pee' zih uss). **Origin:** skull and vertebrae from lambdoidal crest to axis. **Insertion:** clavicle on raphe with clavobrachialis. **Action:** uncertain. 2—**Acromiotrapezius** (uh kroh' mih oh truh pee' zih uss). **Origin:** middorsal line from spinous process of axis to anywhere between first and fourth thoracic vertebrae. Much of the posterior portion is merely a thin aponeurosis lying over the vertebral column and connecting the right and left trapezius muscles without other attachment. Usually considerable fat lies between this aponeurosis and the underlying vertebrae. **Insertion:** metacromion, scapular spine, surface of spinotrapezius. **Action:** moves scapula dorsally. 3—**Spinotrapezius. Origin:** spinous processes of thoracic vertebrae. **Insertion:** scapular spine and fasciae over infraspinatus and supraspinatus. **Action:** draws scapula dorsally and posteriorly.

DELTOIDEUS MUSCLE

represented in the cat by two muscles: **spinodeltoideus, acromiodeltoideus.** It has been suggested that the clavobrachialis is a part of the deltoideus group, then being called the clavodeltoideus, though this has not been generally accepted. 1—**Acromiodeltoideus** (uh kroh' mih oh dell' toyd eh uss). **Origin:** acromion of the spine of the scapula and near-by regions. **Insertion:** humerus, surface of spinodeltoid, with minor attachments on surface of brachialis. **Action:** flexes and rotates humerus. 2—**Spinodeltoideus. Origin:** spine of the scapula and near-by regions. **Insertion:** deltoid ridge of humerus. **Action:** flexes and rotates humerus.

TRICEPS BRACHII MUSCLE

trai' sepps bray' kih ai. **Origin:** three heads—**long head** on scapula, **lateral head** on proximal end of humerus, and **medial head** (Pl. 22 and page opposite) on three regions of the humerus from the proximal to the distal portion. **Insertion:** olecranon and ulna near olecranon. **Action:** extends arm.

plate 24

DEEP MUSCLES OF FORELIMB REGION, LATERAL VIEW

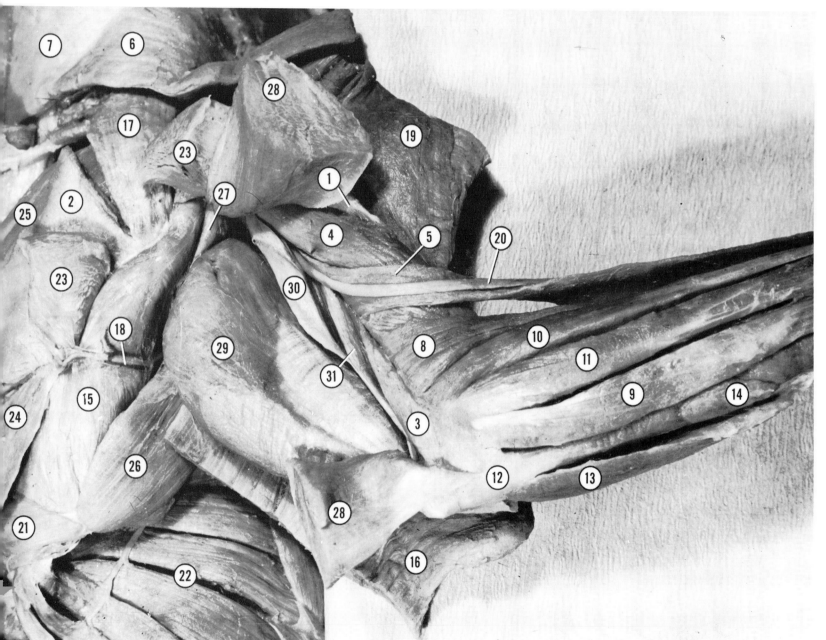

1 acromiodeltoideus
2 acromiotrapezius, cut
3 **anconeus**
4 **brachialis**
5 **brachioradialis**
6 clavobrachialis
7 clavotrapezius
8 **extensor carpi radialis longus**
9 **extensor carpi ulnaris**
10 **extensor digitorum**
11 **extensor digitorum lateralis**
12 **extensor indicis proprius**
13 **flexor carpi ulnaris**
14 **flexor digitorum profundus,** fifth head
15 infraspinatus
16 latissimus dorsi, cut
17 **levator scapulae ventralis**
18 middle subscapular nerve and artery
19 pectoralis major, cut
20 radial nerve, superficial branch
21 rhomboideus
22 serratus ventralis
23 spinodeltoideus, cut
24 spinotrapezius
25 supraspinatus
26 **teres major**
27 **teres minor**
28 **triceps brachii, lateral head,** cut
29 **triceps brachii, long head**
30 **triceps brachii, medial head, long portion**
31 **triceps brachii, medial head, intermediate portion**

plate 24

shows the muscles of the shoulder and arm after the latissimus dorsi, the lateral head of the triceps brachii, and the spinodeltoideus have been cut to show the underlying muscles. Since the lateral head of the triceps brachii is cut, the long and intermediate portions of the medial head can be seen. The third and distal part, known as the short portion of the medial head of the triceps brachii, which was shown on Plate 22, is covered on this side of the arm by the anconeus. The brachialis is shown partly covered by the insertion end of the acromiodeltoideus and the origin end of the brachioradialis.

ANCONEUS MUSCLE

ang koh nee' uss. **Origin:** humerus. **Insertion:** ulna. **Action:** assumed to keep the capsule of the elbow joint taut; may also extend the forearm.

TERES MAJOR MUSCLE

tee' reez—parallel to the lateral border of the scapula. **Origin:** vertebral part of the lateral border of the scapula and adjoining fascia. **Insertion:** humerus by a tendon common with that of the latissimus dorsi. **Action:** rotates and flexes humerus.

TERES MINOR MUSCLE

Origin: lateral border of scapula near the glenoid cavity. **Insertion:** greater tubercle of humerus. **Action:** rotates and flexes humerus. The lateral head of the triceps brachii has its origin between the teres major and the teres minor.

BRACHIORADIALIS MUSCLE

bray' kih oh ray dih ay' liss. **Origin:** humerus near middle region. **Insertion:** styloid process of radius. **Action:** probably flexes forearm, though some say that it also supinates it.

EXTENSOR CARPI RADIALIS LONGUS MUSCLE

karr' pai ray dih ay' liss. **Origin:** humerus. **Insertion:** second metacarpal. **Action:** extends forefoot.

EXTENSOR DIGITORUM MUSCLE

dihj ih toh' rumm. **Origin:** humerus. **Insertion:** middle and distal phalanges of second, third, fourth, and fifth digits. **Action:** extends the four digits on which it inserts.

EXTENSOR DIGITORUM LATERALIS MUSCLE

Origin: humerus. **Insertion:** variable, usually unites with tendons of extensor digitorum. **Action:** extends the digits.

EXTENSOR CARPI ULNARIS MUSCLE

ull nay' riss. **Origin:** two heads—ulna and lateral epicondyle of humerus. **Insertion:** fifth metacarpal. **Action:** extends and adducts forefoot.

EXTENSOR INDICIS MUSCLE

inn' dih sis. **Origin:** ulna. **Insertion:** usually middle phalanx of second digit; sometimes also first or third digit. **Action:** extends second digit.

FLEXOR DIGITORUM PROFUNDUS MUSCLE

Origin: five heads—three on medial epicondyle of humerus, one on radius, one on ulna. **Insertion:** bases of distal phalanges. **Action:** flexes the digits (Pl. 22).

FLEXOR CARPI ULNARIS MUSCLE

Origin: two heads—humerus and olecranon. **Insertion:** pisiform bone of wrist. **Action:** flexes wrist.

plate 25

DEEP MUSCLES OF SHOULDER, DORSAL VIEW

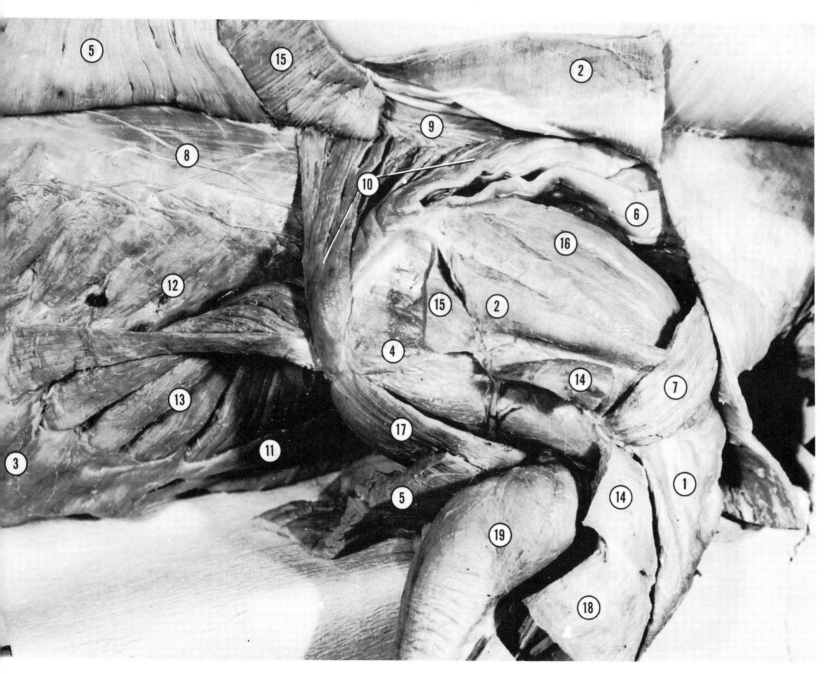

1   acromiodeltoideus
2   acromiotrapezius, cut
3   external abdominal oblique
4   **infraspinatus**
5   latissimus dorsi, cut
6   **levator scapulae dorsalis**
7   **levator scapulae ventralis**
8   lumbodorsal fascia
9   **rhomboideus**, left
10 **rhomboideus**, right
11 scalenus
12 serratus dorsalis anterior
13 serratus ventralis
14 spinodeltoideus, cut
15 spinotrapezius, cut
16 **supraspinatus**
17 teres major
18 triceps brachii, lateral head, cut
19 triceps brachii, long head

plate 25

shows a lateral view of the deep muscles of the shoulder and back. The latissimus dorsi, spinotrapezius, acromiotrapezius, and spinodeltoideus have been cut to expose the deeper muscles.

RHOMBOIDEUS MUSCLE

romm' boydeus—a thick muscle, easily separated into a variable number of parts. **Origin:** middorsal line from posterior half of cervical region to anterior half of thoracic region. **Insertion:** medial border of scapula. **Action:** draws scapula toward middorsal line. This muscle is thought to be homologous to both the rhomboideus major and the rhomboideus minor muscles of man.

LEVATOR SCAPULAE DORSALIS MUSCLE

leh vay' terr skapp' iu lee dor say' liss. **Origin:** lambdoidal ridge under clavotrapezius. **Insertion:** either scapula or surface of levator scapulae near scapula. **Action:** rotates and draws scapula anteriorly. It is thought to be homologous to a part of the human rhomboideus. It lies so close to the rhomboideus in the cat as to be easily mistaken for a part of it but can be recognized by its origin.

LEVATOR SCAPULAE VENTRALIS MUSCLE

venn tray' liss. **Origin:** basioccipital and transverse process of atlas. **Insertion:** metacromion and infraspinous fossa. **Action:** draws scapula anteriorly. This muscle has no homologue in man.

SUPRASPINATUS MUSCLE

siu pruh spai nay' tuss. **Origin:** supraspinatus fossa and anterior surface of subscapularis. **Insertion:** greater tubercle of humerus. **Action:** extends humerus.

INFRASPINATUS MUSCLE

Origin: infraspinatus fossa. **Insertion:** greater tubercle of humerus. **Action:** rotates humerus outward.

plate 26

MUSCLES OF TRUNK REGION, DORSAL VIEW

1 external abdominal oblique, cut
2 external intercostals
3 latissimus dorsi, cut
4 rhomboideus
5 **serratus dorsalis anterior**
6 **serratus dorsalis posterior**
7 **serratus ventralis**
8 spinotrapezius
9 teres major
10 thoracolumbalis fascia

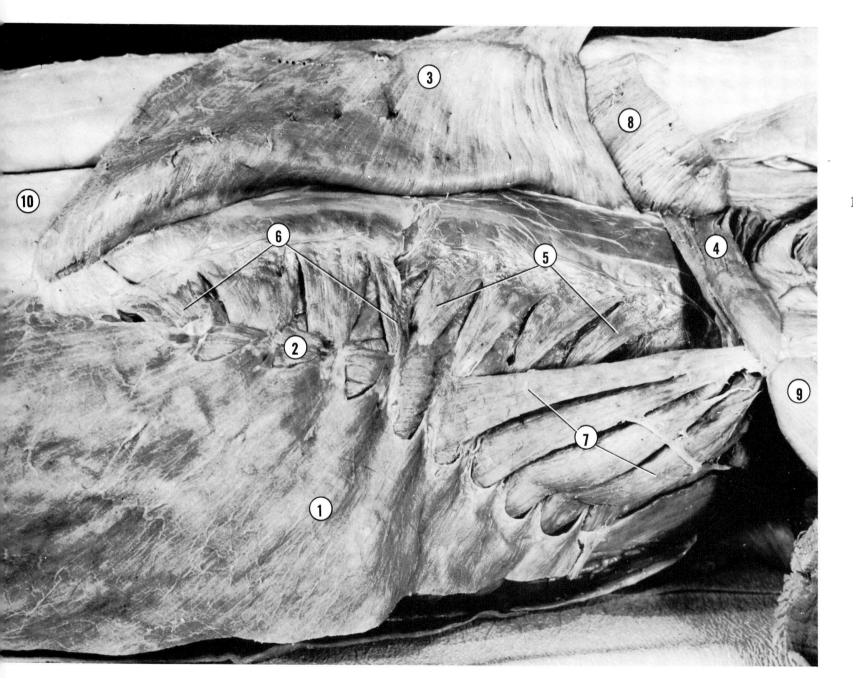

plate 26 shows the dorsal muscles of the thoracic region and the superficial muscles of the abdomen in lateral view. The latissimus dorsi has been cut and turned back and the serratus muscles dissected free from fat and loose connective tissue.

SERRATUS DORSALIS MUSCLE

seh ray′ tuss dor say′ liss—a muscle having numerous heads, which give it a serrated or toothed appearance. It is divided into **serratus dorsalis anterior** and **serratus dorsalis posterior. 1—Serratus dorsalis anterior. Origin:** thoracolumbalis fascia covering the deep muscles of the back and extending to the middorsal line. **Insertion:** first nine to eleven ribs. **Action:** assumed to draw ribs anteriorly. **2—Serratus dorsalis posterior. Origin:** thoracolumbalis fascia over lumbar region, but the parts lie at a different angle from the parts of the serratus dorsalis anterior. **Insertion:** last four or five ribs. **Action:** draws the ribs anteriorly.

plate 27   MUSCLES OF BODY WALL, VENTRAL VIEW

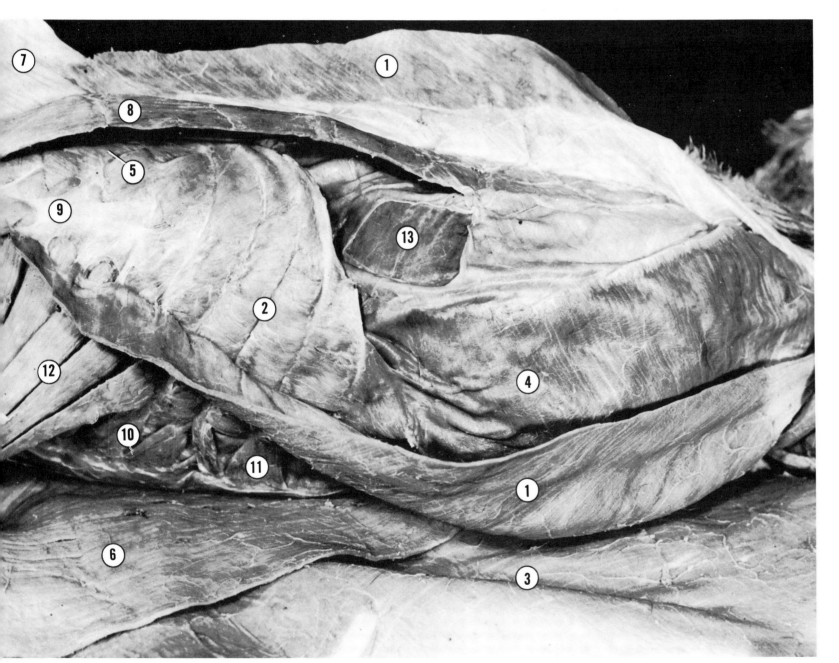

1 **external abdominal oblique,** cut
2 **external intercostals**
3 great cutaneous
4 **internal abdominal oblique**
5 **internal intercostals**
6 latissimus dorsi
7 pectoralis minor, cut
8 **rectus abdominis**
9 **scalenus medius, tendons of origin**
10 serratus dorsalis anterior
11 serratus dorsalis posterior
12 serratus ventralis
13 **transversus abdominis**

plate 27

shows the external abdominal oblique bisected lengthwise and reflected to show underlying abdominal and thoracic muscles. The internal abdominal oblique is seen to terminate in an aponeurosis at some distance from the midventral line. A window has been cut in the aponeurosis of the internal abdominal oblique to show the transversus abdominis underlying the obliques.

EXTERNAL ABDOMINAL OBLIQUE MUSCLE

Origin: last nine or ten ribs and thoracolumbalis fascia (Pl. 26). **Insertion:** by an aponeurosis to the linea alba from sternum to pubis. **Action:** compresses abdominal viscera thereby decreasing volume of abdominal cavity.

INTERNAL ABDOMINAL OBLIQUE MUSCLE

underneath the external abdominal oblique, but with its fasciculi at quite a different angle, thus giving the abdominal wall greater resistance to rupture than if the fasciculi of both layers were parallel. **Origin:** thoracolumbalis fascia in the lumbar and iliac regions. **Insertion:** by a two-layered aponeurosis which lies both over and under the rectus abdominis to the linea alba, with the external abdominal oblique. **Action:** compresses abdominal region thereby decreasing volume of abdominal cavity.

TRANSVERSUS ABDOMINIS MUSCLE

tranns verr' sus abb domm' ih niss—the third, innermost muscle layer of the abdominal wall, with its fasciculi again at an angle similar to those of the external abdominal oblique. **Origin:** ribs, diaphragm, lumbar vertebrae, and ilium. **Insertion:** in the linea alba by a thin aponeurosis which underlies the rectus abdominis. **Action:** constricts abdominal region thereby decreasing volume of abdominal cavity.

RECTUS ABDOMINIS MUSCLE

Origin: pubis. **Insertion:** first and second costal cartilages and sternum. This is largely convention, since anatomists do not always agree on the end which should be called the origin and the end which should be called the insertion (opposite Pl. 16). **Action:** compresses abdominal contents and helps to flex body. The linea alba is composed of the aponeuroses of the external abdominal oblique, internal abdominal oblique and transversus abdominis muscles. The aponeuroses of thèse muscles fuse on the median plane between the two rectus abdominis muscles with those of the opposite side, and their fibers interlace, forming a single tendinous band which extends from the xiphoid process to the pubic symphysis.

INTERCOSTAL MUSCLES

The **external intercostals** are arranged in a direction similar to that of the fasciculi of the external abdominal oblique, while the fasciculi of the **internal intercostals** run in a direction similar to the fasciculi of the internal abdominal oblique. The comparative anatomist considers them to be similar parts of the same hypaxial system. Both are used in breathing. The function of the intercostal muscles has been widely disputed. Recent electromyographic studies of costal respiration in man show that in quiet breathing the external intercostal muscles contract only during inspiration. Expiration is by elastic recoil of the thoracic cage. The muscles are of more importance in working together to keep the intercostal spaces from bulging or caving in during varying intrathoracic pressures, and maintain the constant width of the intercostal spaces during elevation by the scalene muscles or depression by the abdominal muscles. The internal intercostals may usually be seen without dissection of the external intercostals near the sternum between the more posterior costal cartilages and just under the rectus abdominis, where the external intercostals end in thin transparent membranes which attach to the sternum.

plate 28

SUPERFICIAL MUSCLES OF THIGH, MEDIAL VIEW

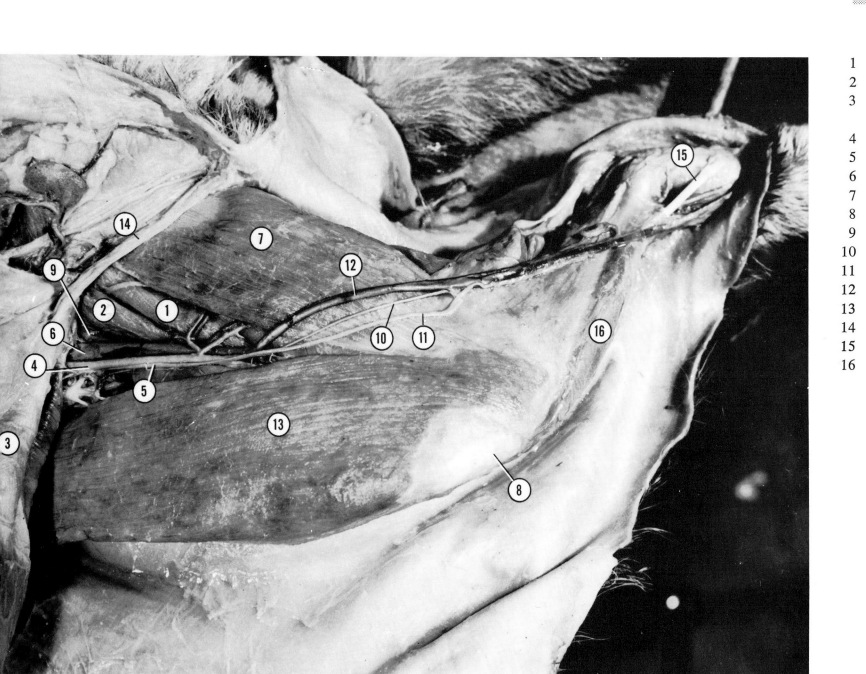

1   adductor femoris
2   **adductor longus**
3   aponeurosis of external abdominal
    oblique
4   femoral artery
5   femoral nerve
6   femoral vein
7   **gracilis**
8   patella
9   pectineus
10 saphenous artery
11 saphenous nerve
12 saphenous vein
13 **sartorius**
14 spermatic cord
15 tendon of tibialis anterior
16 tibialis anterior

plate 28 shows the skin dissected away from the medial surface of the right hind leg to expose those structures immediately underneath. Since the specimen used was a male, the right and left spermatic cords can be seen close to the pubic symphysis, where, in the intact specimen, they are found directly under the skin and superficial to the muscles. The spermatic cord emerges from the abdominal cavity through the superficial inguinal ring in the external abdominal oblique muscle and ends in the scrotum, a pocket of skin containing the testes (Pl. 41 and page opposite).

SARTORIUS MUSCLE

sarr toh′ rih uss. **Origin:** ilium. **Insertion:** tibia, patella, and fascia of knee. **Action:** adducts and rotates femur and extends lower part of leg.

GRACILIS MUSCLE

grass′ ih liss. **Origin:** posterior portion of symphysis of pubis and ischium. **Insertion:** medial surface of tibia by an aponeurosis. **Action:** adducts and flexes leg.

ADDUCTOR LONGUS MUSCLE

Origin: pubis. **Insertion:** femur. **Action:** adducts thigh.

ADDUCTOR FEMORIS MUSCLE

femm′ oh riss. **Origin:** pubis and ischium. **Insertion:** femur. **Action:** adducts thigh; probably flexes toward trunk. This muscle is said to be homologous to both the adductor magnus and the adductor brevis of man.

plate 29

MUSCLES OF THIGH, MEDIAL VIEW

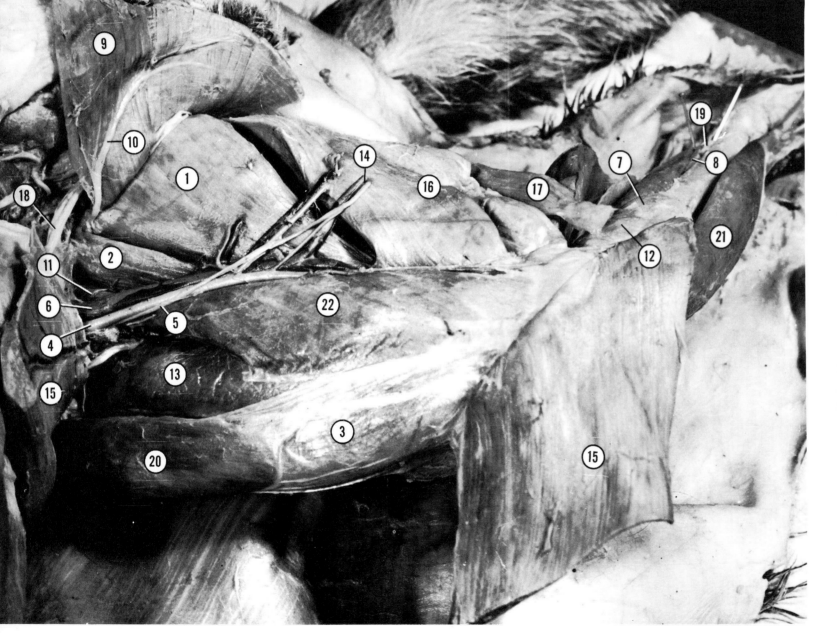

1 **adductor femoris**
2 adductor longus
3 fascia lata
4 femoral artery
5 femoral nerve
6 femoral vein
7 **flexor digitorum longus**
8 **flexor hallucis longus**
9 gracilis, cut
10 obturator nerve
11 **pectineus**
12 **popliteus**
13 rectus femoris of quadriceps femoris
14 saphenous artery, nerve, and vein, cut ends
15 sartorius, cut
16 **semimembranosus**
17 **semitendinosus**
18 spermatic cord
19 **tendon of tibialis posterior**
20 **tensor fasciae latae**
21 **tibialis anterior**
22 vastus medialis of quadriceps femoris

plate 29

shows the sartorius and gracilis muscles cut to expose the deeper muscles. The saphenous artery, nerve, and vein have been cut and almost entirely removed, leaving the proximal ends lying across the semimembranosus muscle. A pin separates the tendon of the flexor hallucis longus from the tendon of the tibialis posterior, which lies against the tibia, while the popliteus is visible only because the semitendinosus has had its insertion cut from the bone and is slightly displaced posteriorly.

PECTINEUS MUSCLE

peck tinn' eh uss. **Origin:** pubis. **Insertion:** femur. **Action:** adducts thigh.

SEMIMEMBRANOSUS MUSCLE

semm ih memm bruh noh' sus. **Origin:** ischium. **Insertion:** femur and tibia. **Action:** extends thigh.

SEMITENDINOSUS MUSCLE

semm ih tenn dih noh' sus. **Origin:** tuberosity of ischium. **Insertion:** tibia. **Action:** flexes shank on thigh.

POPLITEUS MUSCLE

popp litt' eh uss. **Origin:** lateral epicondyle of femur. **Insertion:** tibia. **Action:** rotates thigh to turn toes inward.

TIBIALIS POSTERIOR MUSCLE

tibb ih ay' liss poss tee' rih or. **Origin:** fibula and tibia. **Insertion:** navicular and intermediate cuneiform. **Action:** extends foot. Found immediately posterior to tibia and deep to the more superficial muscles.

TIBIALIS ANTERIOR MUSCLE

Origin: tibia, fibula, and interosseous membrane. **Insertion:** first metatarsal. **Action:** flexes foot.

FLEXOR DIGITORUM LONGUS MUSCLE

Origin: tibia and fibula. **Insertion:** distal phalanges of all four digits. **Action:** flexes toes.

FLEXOR HALLUCIS LONGUS MUSCLE

hah liu' sis. **Origin:** tibia, fibula, interosseus membrane, and near-by muscles. **Insertion:** tendon of flexor digitorum longus to distal phalanges of all four digits. **Action:** flexes toes.

TENSOR FASCIAE LATAE MUSCLE

fassh' ih ee lay' tee. **Origin:** fascia lata covering gluteus medius. **Insertion:** fascia lata. **Action:** tenses fascia lata and flexes thigh.

plate 30

DEEP MUSCLES OF THIGH, MEDIAL VIEW

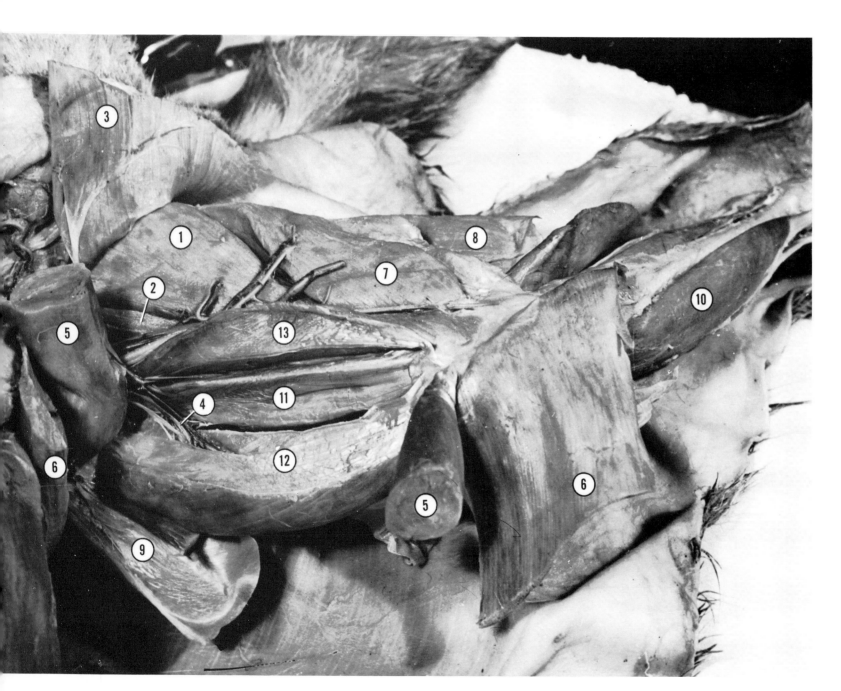

1 adductor femoris
2 adductor longus
3 gracilis, cut
4 lateral circumflex femoral artery and vein
5 **rectus femoris** of **quadriceps femoris, cut**
6 sartorius, cut
7 semimembranosus
8 semitendinosus
9 tensor fasciae latae
10 tibialis anterior
11 **vastus intermedius** of **quadriceps femoris**
12 **vastus lateralis** of **quadriceps femoris**
13 **vastus medialis** of **quadriceps femoris**

plate 30 shows the fascia lata cut and the underlying parts of the quadriceps femoris muscle exposed and separated. The rectus femoris has been cut and the ends turned back to show the vastus intermedius. In some specimens it is easy to separate the vastus intermedius from the vastus lateralis and vastus medialis, while in other specimens they are so well united by connective tissue that separation is almost impossible.

QUADRICEPS FEMORIS MUSCLE

kwodd' rih sepps femm' oh riss. **Origin:** The four large heads are almost separate muscles: **1—rectus femoris,** ilium near acetabulum. **2—vastus lateralis,** femur near greater trochanter. **3—vastus medialis,** femur. **4—vastus intermedius,** shaft of femur. **Insertion:** tuberosity of tibia, by a strong tendon in which the patella is found as a sesamoid bone. **Action:** extends leg. It is a very powerful extensor muscle and is assumed to be homologous to the triceps brachii of the arm.

plate 31   SUPERFICIAL MUSCLES OF THIGH, LATERAL VIEW

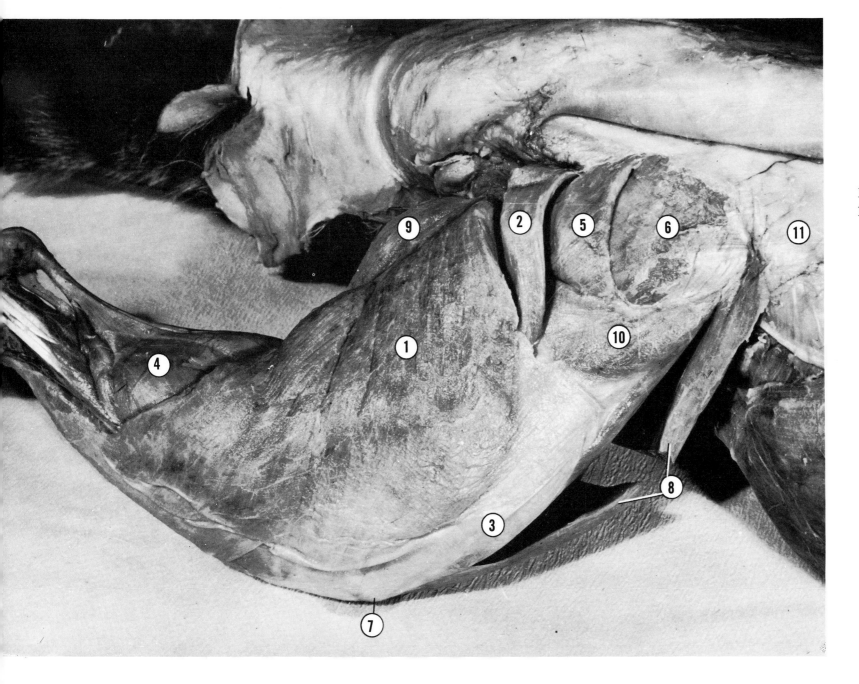

1 **biceps femoris**
2 **caudofemoralis**
3 fascia lata
4 gastrocnemius
5 **gluteus maximus**
6 **gluteus medius**
7 patella
8 sartorius, cut
9 semitendinosus
10 **tensor fasciae latae**
11 thoracolumbalis fascia

plate 31

shows the lateral superficial muscles of the thigh. The fascia over the gluteus medius has been partially dissected away. The gluteus maximus and tensor fasciae latae are usually practically continuous near the insertion of the gluteus maximus.

BICEPS FEMORIS MUSCLE

bai' sepps femm' oh riss. **Origin:** tuberosity of ischium. **Insertion:** patella and tibia. **Action:** flexes shank and abducts thigh.

CAUDOFEMORALIS MUSCLE

kah doh femm oh ray' liss. **Origin:** transverse processes of second and third caudal vertebrae. **Insertion:** lateral border of patella. **Action:** abducts thigh, aids in extending shank, and pulls tail laterally.

GLUTEUS MEDIUS MUSCLE

gloo tee' uss mee' dih uss. **Origin:** ilium, transverse processes of last sacral and first caudal vertebrae, and fasciae over sacral and caudal vertebrae. **Insertion:** greater trochanter. **Action:** abducts thigh.

GLUTEUS MAXIMUS MUSCLE

Origin: transverse processes of last sacral and first caudal vertebrae and near-by thoracolumbalis fasciae. **Insertion:** greater trochanter and femur. **Action:** abducts thigh. It is called the gluteus maximus because it is homologous to the gluteus maximus of man, but it is a relatively small muscle in the cat.

FASCIA LATA

fassh' ih uh lay' tuh. **Origin:** sacrum, caudal vertebrae, and ilium. Passes over gluteus medius and gluteus maximus. **Insertion:** border of vastus medialis, tendon of biceps femoris, patella. **Function:** in addition to the usual functions of fasciae, such as investing various muscles, forming intermuscular septa which separates groups of muscles, blending with ligaments, and attaching to subcutaneous bony prominences, the fascia lata may aid circulation indirectly as it prevents stagnation of blood in the veins of the thigh by maintaining pressure on the walls of the veins.

TENSOR FASCIAE LATAE MUSCLE

fassh' ih ee lay' tee. **Origin:** fascia lata. **Insertion:** fascia lata. **Action:** keeps fascia lata taut.

plate 32   MUSCLES OF SHANK AND DEEP MUSCLES OF THIGH, LATERAL VIEW

1   adductor femoris
2   biceps femoris, cut
3   **caudofemoralis**
4   common peroneal nerve
5   **extensor digitorum longus**
6   fascia lata
7   **flexor hallucis longus**
8   **gastrocnemius**
9   gluteus maximus
10   gluteus medius
11   **peroneus brevis**
12   **peroneus longus**
13   **peroneus tertius**
14   **plantaris**
15   sartorius, cut
16   sciatic nerve
17   semimembranosus
18   semitendinosus
19   **soleus**
20   tensor fasciae latae
21   **tenuissimus**
22   tibial nerve
23   **tibialis anterior**

plate 32 shows the biceps femoris muscle cut to expose the underlying muscles. The tendons of the caudofemoralis and the tenuissimus muscles, which appear to be separate, are actually very close to the biceps femoris and, unless they are first dissected free, will be cut when the biceps femoris is cut. The sciatic nerve is shown as it divides into the common peroneal and tibial nerves.

TENUISSIMUS MUSCLE

tenn iu iss' ih muss. **Origin:** transverse process of second caudal vertebra. **Insertion:** fascia of biceps femoris. **Action:** assumed to aid in flexing leg.

GASTROCNEMIUS MUSCLE

gass trock nee' mih uss. **Origin:** two heads—lateral head on patella, femur, lateral sesamoid, and fasciae; medial head on femur and lateral sesamoid. **Insertion:** calcaneus, by strong tendo calcaneus. **Action:** extends foot.

PERONEUS LONGUS MUSCLE

perr oh nee' uss. **Origin:** lateral surface of fibula. **Insertion:** bases of metatarsals. **Action:** pronates and flexes foot.

PERONEUS BREVIS MUSCLE

bree' viss. **Origin:** distal half of fibula. **Insertion:** fifth metatarsal, base of lateral surface. **Action:** extends foot.

PERONEUS TERTIUS MUSCLE

terr' shih uss. **Origin:** fibula, lateral surface. **Insertion:** lateral border of extensor tendon of fifth digit between first and second phalanges. **Action:** extends and abducts fifth digit and flexes foot.

PLANTARIS MUSCLE

plann tay' riss. **Origin:** lateral border of patella, lateral sesamoid, and femur. **Insertion:** calcaneus by tendon, which is sheathed by the tendo calcaneus. **Action:** extends foot.

SOLEUS MUSCLE

soh' leh uss. **Origin:** lateral head and border of fibula. **Insertion:** calcaneus by lateral border of tendo calcaneus. **Action:** extends foot.

FLEXOR HALLUCIS LONGUS MUSCLE

hah liu' sis. **Origin:** tibia, fibula, interosseus membrane, and near-by muscles. **Insertion:** bases of distal phalanges of foot. **Action:** flexes toes.

EXTENSOR DIGITORUM LONGUS MUSCLE

Origin: lateral epicondyle of femur. **Insertion:** bases of second phalanges on dorsal side of foot. **Action:** extends phalanges.

TIBIALIS ANTERIOR MUSCLE

tibb ih ay' liss. **Origin:** tibia, fibula, and interosseus membrane. **Insertion:** first metatarsal. **Action:** flexes foot.

plate 33 ABDOMINAL ORGANS

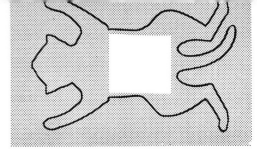

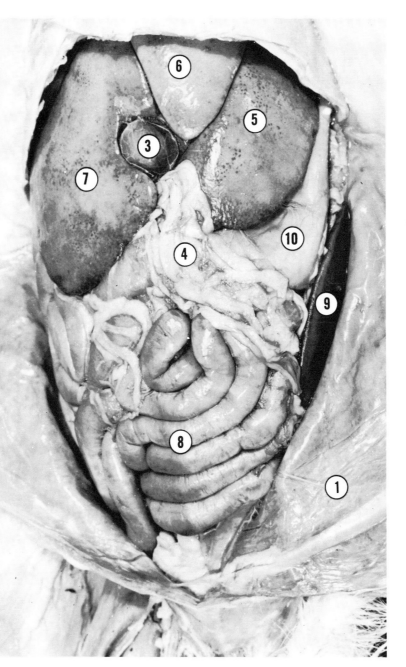

1 body wall
2 falciform ligament
3 **gall bladder**
4 **greater omentum**
5 liver, left lateral lobe
6 liver, left medial lobe
7 liver, right medial lobe
8 small intestine
9 **spleen**
10 **stomach**

plate 33

shows two cats with the body wall cut along the linea alba and turned back to expose the viscera *in situ*. These two cats were chosen to show the great variations that occur in the size and location of various organs. In the cat on the left the greater omentum covers almost the entire small intestine, the gall bladder is just barely visible, and the liver and spleen completely cover the stomach; while in the other cat the greater omentum is small and covers very little of the small intestine, the gall bladder is quite prominent, and the stomach is easily seen.

PERITONEUM

a serous membrane lining the abdominal cavity and consisting of a thin layer of connective tissue supporting an epithelium. The layer of peritoneum lining the body wall is known as the **parietal peritoneum,** while that which surrounds the organs lying in the body cavity is known as the **visceral peritoneum.** No organs actually lie in the peritoneal cavity, since that cavity is between the parietal peritoneum and the visceral peritoneum, which are in contact with each other with just enough serous peritoneal fluid to lubricate their surfaces. The peritoneal cavity is a part of the celom, which also includes the two pleural cavities and the pericardial cavity.

LIVER

varies in shape but shows right and left divisions, demonstrated by the position of the **falciform ligament.** Each right and left lobe generally divides into medial and lateral portions, with further subdivision of the right lateral portion into three parts. One of these, the small **caudate lobe,** is located dorsal to the lesser omentum of the stomach. The **gall bladder** functions as a storage reservoir for bile formed by the liver. Bile may empty directly through **hepatic ducts** to the **common bile duct** to the duodenum, or it may pass up the **cystic duct** to the gall bladder, where it is stored until needed, at which time it passes through the cystic duct to the bile duct to the duodenum (Pl. 48).

MESENTERIES

consist of a sheet of connective tissue covered by visceral peritoneum on both sides and usually containing blood vessels and nerves. Mesenteries are either middorsal, midventral, or lateral. The middorsal and midventral mesenteries develop in the embryo connected to the gut. During growth the midventral mesentery disappears almost entirely, while the middorsal mesentery gives rise to most of the mesenteries of the digestive system. Lateral mesenteries develop as the organs grow from the body wall toward the center of the body cavity, carrying the peritoneum with them. In the cat the principal mesenteries are as follows:

1—**midventral mesenteries**
   a—**falciform ligament,** separates right and left lobes of liver, between liver and linea alba.
   b—**lesser omentum,** between liver, duodenum, and lesser curvature of stomach. Divided into hepatogastric ligament and hepatoduodenal ligament.
   c—**ligamentum teres hepatis,** the remains of umbilical vein in edge of falciform ligament.
   d—**suspensory ligament,** attaches urinary bladder to linea alba.

2—**middorsal mesenteries**
   a—**greater omentum,** from greater curvature of stomach to dorsal body wall. Between spleen and stomach it is called the **gastrolienal ligament.**
   b—**mesentery proper,** to small intestine.
   c—**mesocolon,** to colon.
   d—**mesorectum,** to rectum.

3—**lateral mesenteries**
   a—**triangular ligament,** from left lobe of liver to diaphragm. A right triangular ligament is also sometimes present.
   b—**hepatorenal ligament,** from right lateral lobe of liver to right kidney.
   c—**lateral ligaments,** to the urinary bladder.
   d—**broad ligament** of uterus.
   e—**round ligament** of uterus.

plate 34

EPIPLOIC FORAMEN AND ABDOMINAL ORGANS

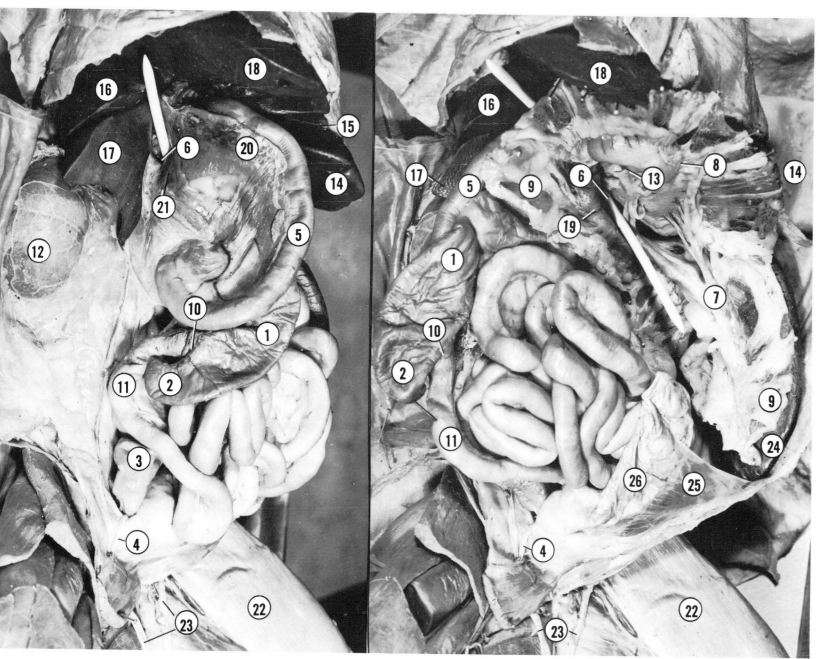

1 ascending colon
2 cecum
3 descending colon
4 ductus deferens
5 duodenum
6 **epiploic foramen**
7 gastrolienal ligament
8 greater curvature of stomach
9 **greater omentum**
10 **ileocolic junction**
11 ileum
12 kidney, right
13 lesser curvature of stomach
14 liver, left lateral lobe
15 liver, left medial lobe
16 liver, right lateral lobe, anterior portion
17 liver, right lateral lobe, posterior portion
18 liver, right medial lobe
19 **pancreas, left lobe**
20 **pancreas, right lobe**
21 portal vein
22 sartorius muscle
23 spermatic cord
24 spleen
25 **suspensory ligament of urinary bladder**
26 urinary bladder

plate 34

shows a curved white probe in the epiploic foramen. In the picture on the left the medial lobes of the liver have been pulled anteriorly, the duodenum and rest of the small intestine have been lifted toward the left side of the cat, and a probe has been inserted into the epiploic foramen. Lymph nodes, fat, and connective tissue have been dissected away from the cecum and the ileocolic junction. In the picture on the right the omental bursa has been opened by removing the greater omentum to within about an inch of its attachments to the stomach, spleen, and left lobe of pancreas, which has grown into the greater omentum near its attachment to the dorsal body wall. The edges of the greater omentum have been pinned back to demonstrate that it is a closed, saclike mesentery, with the epiploic foramen as its opening. The end of the probe nearer the center of the picture would be inside the sac if it were still intact. The urinary bladder has been pulled slightly to the right to show both the suspensory ligament and the right lateral ligament, which encloses a mass of fat. In this photograph the cecum and ileocolic junction have been displaced slightly to the right of the cat. It should be noted that the picture on the right shows the left lobe of the pancreas, while the picture on the left shows the right lobe of the pancreas.

GREATER OMENTUM

in the cat folds to form the **lesser peritoneal sac** or **omental bursa.** It has only one opening, the **epiploic foramen.** In the fetus the stomach rotates its dorsal edge to the left, thereby changing the position of its dorsal and ventral mesenteries. The dorsal mesentery grows to a size out of all proportion to its supporting function, which causes it to fold into the lesser peritoneal sac. The **spleen** is contained between the two peritoneal layers of the **greater omentum,** and that portion of the greater omentum between stomach and spleen is called the **gastrolienal ligament.** The liver grows between the two layers of the ventral mesentery, the larger and dorsal part of the ventral mesentery being left between the lesser curvature of the stomach and liver as the **lesser omentum** and the ventral part being left as the **falciform ligament** of the liver between body wall and liver.

EPIPLOIC FORAMEN

epp ih ploh′ ick—opens into the lesser peritoneal sac from the **greater peritoneal cavity** or peritoneal cavity proper. It is bounded anteriorly by the caudate lobe of the liver covered by the lesser omentum, ventrally by the portal vein and bile duct, dorsally by the dorsal body wall, and posteriorly by the mesentery proper.

DIGESTIVE SYSTEM

includes **alimentary canal** or **gut** and its **glands.** The alimentary canal consists of the following parts in order: mouth, oral cavity, pharynx, esophagus, stomach, small intestine, large intestine, and anus. The glands external to the canal are the salivary glands (Pl. 51), the liver, and the pancreas.

STOMACH

a dilated portion of the gut, chiefly for the storage of food until it can be admitted in small amounts into the duodenum. It communicates with the esophagus at the **cardiac orifice** and extends to the **pyloric orifices,** which is the opening into the duodenum surrounded by the strong **pyloric sphincter muscle.** The **lesser omentum** is attached to the lesser curvature on the right and the **greater omentum** to the greater curvature on the left.

PANCREAS

the most important digestive gland, with left and right lobes. The duodenum receives the **pancreatic duct** and the **common bile duct,** which open in a common orifice on the duodenal papilla (Pl. 48).

SMALL INTESTINE

consists of **1—duodenum** (diu oh dee′ numm), **2—jejunum** (jeh joo′ numm), and **3—ileum** (ill′ eh umm). There is no definite boundary between these three regions, though the **duodenum** is the shortest, supposedly ending as the intestinal loop, shown in this photograph, turns posteriorly. The **jejunum** is arbitrarily defined as the first two-fifths and the **ileum** as the last three-fifths of the remainder of the small intestine.

LARGE INTESTINE

divided into **cecum, ascending colon, transverse colon, descending colon,** and **rectum.** The cecum (Pl. 42) is that portion projecting posteriorly from the ileocolic junction, without vermiform appendix in the cat. The rectum extends directly posteriorly, middorsally, and lies mostly within the pelvis.

plate 35

ABDOMINAL ORGANS IN PREGNANCY; HORNS OF UTERUS INTACT

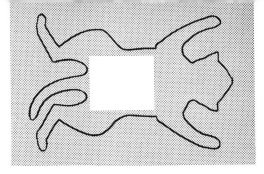

1 body wall
2 greater omentum over intestine
3 liver
4 stomach
5 suspensory ligament of urinary bladder
6 thorax
7 urinary bladder
8 **uterus, body**
9 **uterus, left horn**
10 **uterus, right horn**

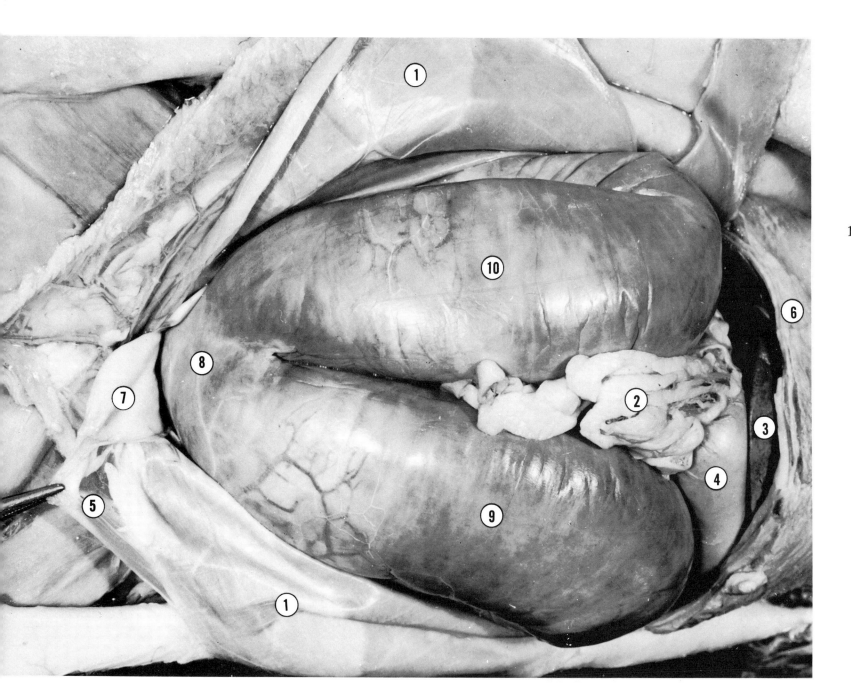

plate 35

shows the body wall opened along the linea alba and the horns of the uterus left intact to demonstrate their appearance in pregnancy as compared with those of the normal female (Pl. 40).

FETAL DEVELOPMENT

The mammalian embryo develops four **fetal** or **extra-embryonic membranes** soon after early cleavage of the fertilized egg, namely, the **chorion, amnion, allantois,** and **yolk sac.** The period of **gestation** in the cat is about nine weeks, and the fetuses shown in Plates 35–39 would have been born in a few more days. At birth the amnion and chorion are usually broken by the uterine contractions. Since the head typically is directed toward the outside, it is forced out first, then the kitten is passed out, dragging with it placenta and fetal membranes still attached to the umbilical cord; the placenta plus the fetal membranes are usually called the **afterbirth.** As the kitten takes its first breath, the blood is drawn into the vessels of the pulmonary system, reducing the amount of blood for the allantoic vessels. Consequently, when the mother bites off the umbilical cord, there is little loss of blood.

CHORION

koh′ rih on—the outermost fetal membrane; therefore makes all connections with the environment, namely, the maternal uterus. In the cat it fuses with the outer layer of the allantois to form the **allantochorion.**

AMNION

amm′ nih on—the innermost fetal membrane; thin, and secretes **amniotic fluid,** which protects the fetus against jars, friction, or other injury.

ALLANTOIS

ah lann′ toh iss—an evagination of the hindgut. Its principal function is to take blood vessels to the chorion, while its base usually forms the mammalian urinary bladder. It is large in the cat and, after the very early stages of development, completely fills the space between chorion and amnion. Its outer wall fuses with the chorion to produce an allantochorion (ah lann′ toh koh′ rih on), and its inner wall fuses with the amnion.

YOLK SAC

functionless, but indicates that the premammalian ancestor, presumably reptilian, had large-yolked eggs. It is relatively large at first, but rapidly becomes insignificant and too small to dissect, lying mostly within the umbilical cord.

PLACENTA

that region consisting of a variably intimate relationship of the maternal uterine mucosa with the embryonic chorion. In the cat the placenta is of the zonary type, extending as a band around the approximate center of the chorion. Here the chorion extends many microscopic processes, which lie next to the blood vessels and connective tissue of the maternal mucosa. The mixture is so intimate in the cat and in all mammals with a true placenta that, when the chorion is expelled from the uterus at birth or removed by dissection (Pls. 36 and 39), much of the maternal uterine mucosa is torn away. At birth this causes uterine bleeding, followed by the growth of a new mucosal surface.

UMBILICAL CORD

connects the fetus with its own fetal membranes, not with the mother (Pl. 38). The fetal blood, formed by the mesoderm of the fetus, is pumped by the heart of the fetus out into the blood vessels of the allantochorionic membrane, where the blood lies near the maternal vessels in the uterine mucosa. Here the fetal blood receives oxygen from, and gives up carbon dioxide to, the maternal blood and also receives food molecules and gives up metabolic wastes; all these functions are accomplished by simple molecular diffusion through several layers of cells. There is never any normal flow of blood directly between mother and offspring.

plate 36

UTERUS OPENED, WITH FETUS IN CHORION

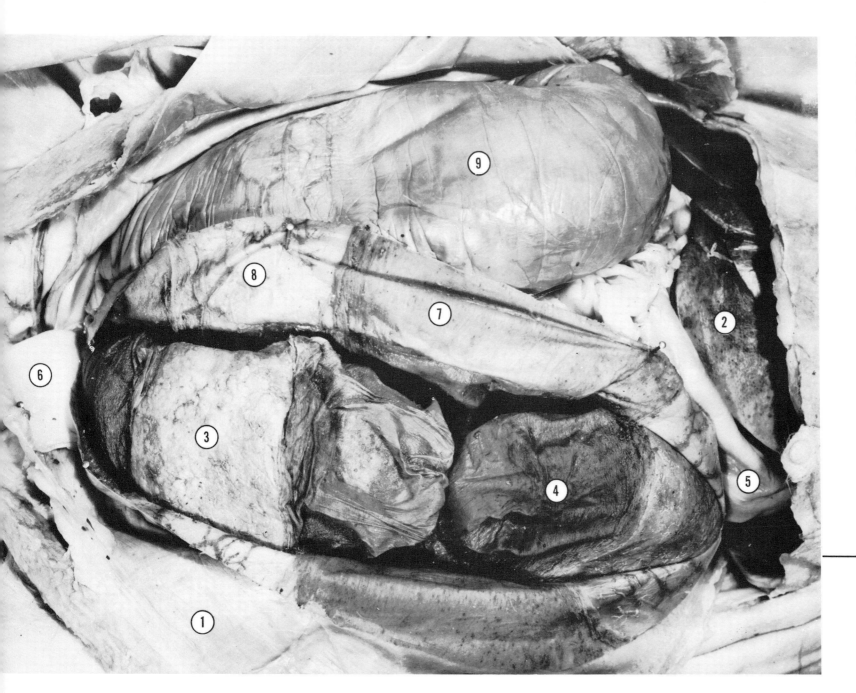

1 body wall
2 liver
3 **placenta**
4 second fetus in its chorion
5 stomach
6 urinary bladder
7 **uterus, mucosa intact**
8 **uterus, mucosa torn away,** exposing muscular layer
9 uterus, right horn

Plate 36 shows the left horn of the uterus opened, exposing an entire fetus in its chorion on the left, with its placenta torn away from the uterine wall. The head of another fetus in its chorion is shown on the right.

plate 37   CHORION OPENED, WITH FETUS IN AMNION

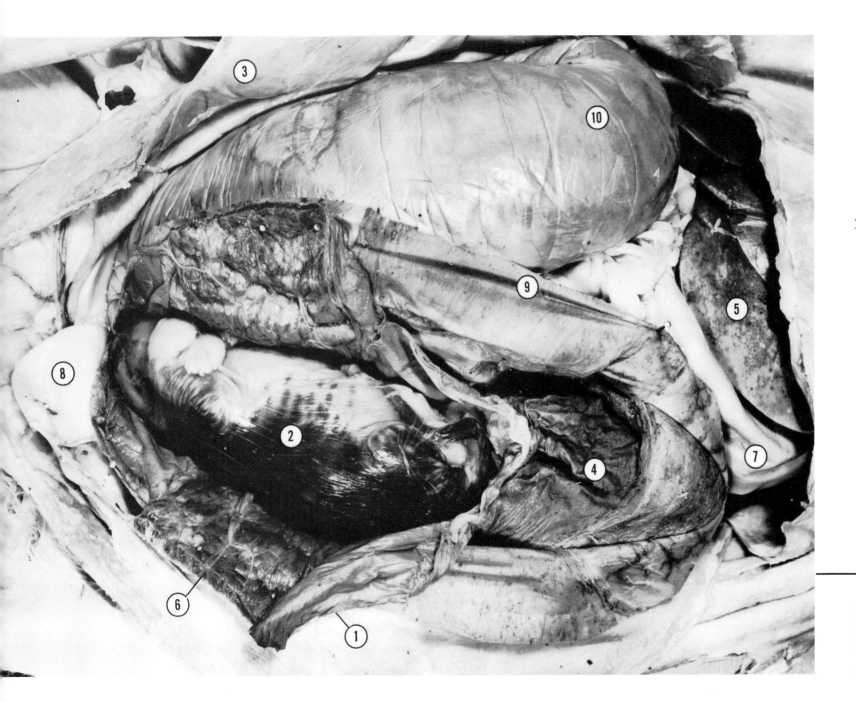

1   allantochorion, cut edge
2   **allantois fused to amnion,** enclosing fetus
3   body wall
4   fetus, still in chorion
5   liver
6   **placenta, cut edge**
7   stomach
8   urinary bladder
9   uterus, cut edge of left horn
10 uterus, right horn

Plate 37 shows the allantochorion opened, with the fetus in its amnion fused with the inner layer of allantois; the fetus on the right is still in its chorion.

plate 38

1 **allantochorion**
2 allantochorion, cut edge
3 amnion, cut edge rolled for clarity
4 amnion fused with inner layer of allantois
5 fetus
6 **placenta**
7 placenta, cut edge (note thickness)
8 **umbilical cord**

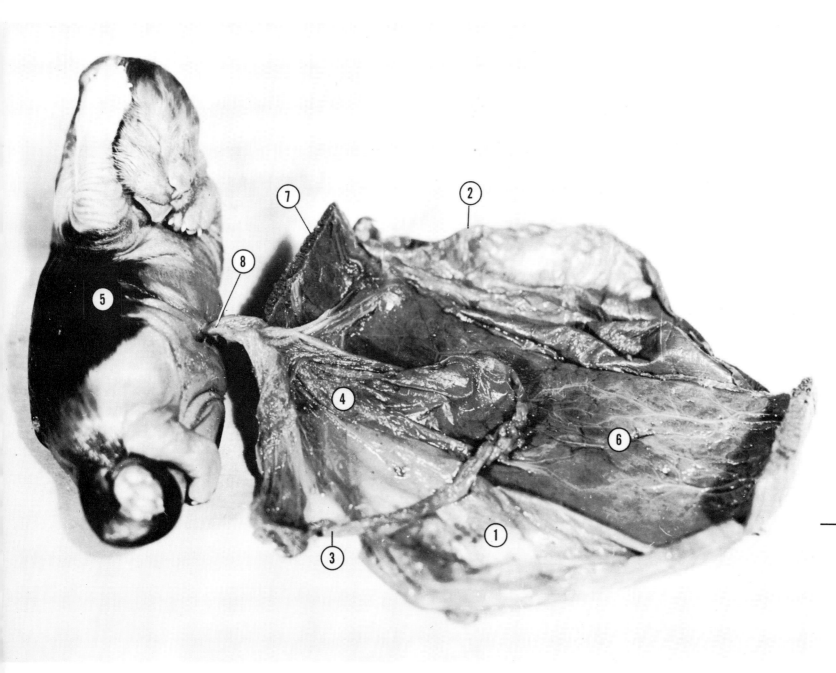

Plate 38 shows the fetus and its membranes completely removed from the uterus to demonstrate the umbilical cord, allantochorion with placenta, and amnion fused with allantois, the edge of which has been rolled slightly to make it more obvious.

plate 39　FETUS WITH MEMBRANES INTACT, REMOVED FROM UTERUS

1 chorion, fused with outer layer of allantois
2 placenta, chorion plus maternal mucosa, zonary type

Plate 39 shows the fetus after it has been removed from the uterus with the fetal membranes intact. The thick zonary placenta, composed of microscopic chorionic villi and hypertrophied uterine mucosa, is shown.

plate 40

FEMALE UROGENITAL SYSTEM

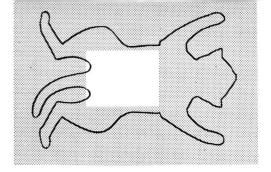

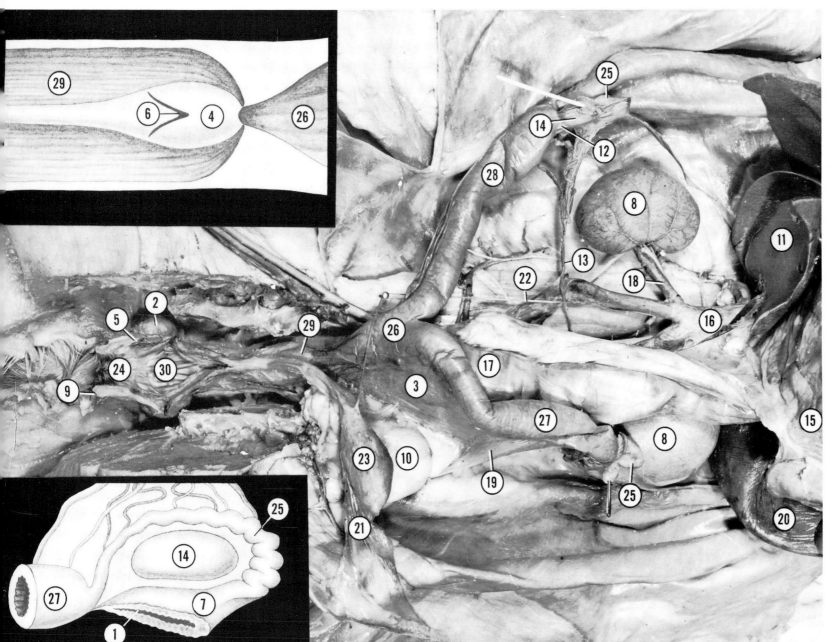

1 **abdominal ostium**
2 anal gland
3 **broad ligament**
4 **cervix of uterus**
5 **clitoris**
6 **external uterine orifice**
7 **infundibulum**
8 kidney
9 labium
10 lateral ligament of bladder, fat-filled
11 liver
12 ovarian ligament
13 ovarian vein
14 **ovary**
15 pancreas
16 posterior vena cava
17 rectum
18 renal vein
19 **round ligament**
20 spleen
21 suspensory ligament
22 ureter
23 urinary bladder
24 urogenital orifice
25 **uterine tube**
26 **uterus, body**
27 **uterus, left horn**
28 **uterus, right horn**
29 **vagina**
30 **vestibule**

plate 40

shows the pelvis opened by removing ventral portions of the ossa coxae to expose the vagina, urethra, and vestibule. The left horn of the uterus has been pulled medially, to demonstrate the uterine tube, the broad ligament, and the round ligament with its mesentery connecting it to the broad ligament. On the right side the ovary is shown in its normal position, with a white probe inserted into the abdominal ostium at the lateral side of the ovary. The uterus in this photograph was slightly dilated with fluid, making it more conspicuous. A more nearly typical, undilated horn of the uterus is shown in Plate 49. The left kidney is in position behind the peritoneum, while the peritoneum, surrounding fat, and surrounding capsule have been dissected away from the right kidney, which has been displaced posteriorly. Its ureter has been freed of fat and pinned to show it passing under the horn of the uterus and entering the urinary bladder. The ureter normally passes laterally rather than medially to the vena cava. The urinary bladder has been displaced to the left with its suspensory ligament. One detail inset shows the vestibule, vagina, and body of the uterus opened to expose the unopened cervix and external uterine orifice, and a second inset shows the abdominal ostium with ovary and uterine tube.

OVARIES

produce **ova** in **ovarian follicles.** At ovulation the ova break out of the follicles through the ovarian epithelium into the celom, where they usually enter the **abdominal ostium** of the **uterine tube.** The abdominal ostium is on the edge of the lateral ligament, lateral to the ovary. After ovulation the follicle cells divide to produce a **corpus luteum** (kor′ puss liu′ teh umm), which is a temporary endocrine gland. If pregnancy occurs, the corpus luteum enlarges and becomes functional, atrophying after the birth of the young.

UTERINE TUBE

region between abdominal ostium and horn of uterus. The tube is ciliated, widening into a ciliated funnel, the **infundibulum,** which surrounds the abdominal ostium. Presumably the current created by the cilia is sufficient to suck the ova into the abdominal ostium, to create the current against which the spermatozoa swim, and to push the ova slowly into the horn of the uterus after they are fertilized. Fertilization in mammals normally takes place in the uterine tube near the abdominal ostium.

UTERUS

divided into **right** and **left horns** and a median **body.** The fetuses develop in the horns, and the body serves only as a passageway in animals that typically give birth to several young at one time.

VAGINA

region between uterus and vestibule; receives the penis of the male at copulation. The uterus projects slightly into the vagina as the **cervix** or neck of the uterus, appearing to be continuous with the long, pointed ridge of uncertain function on the dorsal side of the vagina. The V-shaped **external uterine orifice** is located at the posterior end of the cervix. In man the cervix frequently is the site of tumors and infections.

OVARIAN LIGAMENT

short, tough; attaches ovary to horn of uterus.

BROAD LIGAMENT

mesentery along lateral side of entire uterus, connecting it to body wall.

ROUND LIGAMENT

in the cat it is a fibrous cord, extending between uterus and labial swelling of the vulva and found in the free edge of a flat mesentery connecting the round ligament to the broad ligament and somewhat at right angles to it. It is homologous to the gubernaculum, the fetal structure in the male that connects the testis to the peritoneal sac in the scrotum.

VESTIBULE

short common passageway for excretory and reproductive systems into which vagina and urethra enter. It ends in the **urogenital orifice** surrounded by the labia, which are homologous to the scrotum. At the anterior end of the urogenital orifice is a minute projection containing erectile tissue, the **clitoris,** which is homologous to the penis of the male.

KIDNEYS

opposite Plate 42.

URETER

opposite Plate 42.

URINARY BLADDER

opposite Plate 42.

plate 41   MALE UROGENITAL SYSTEM

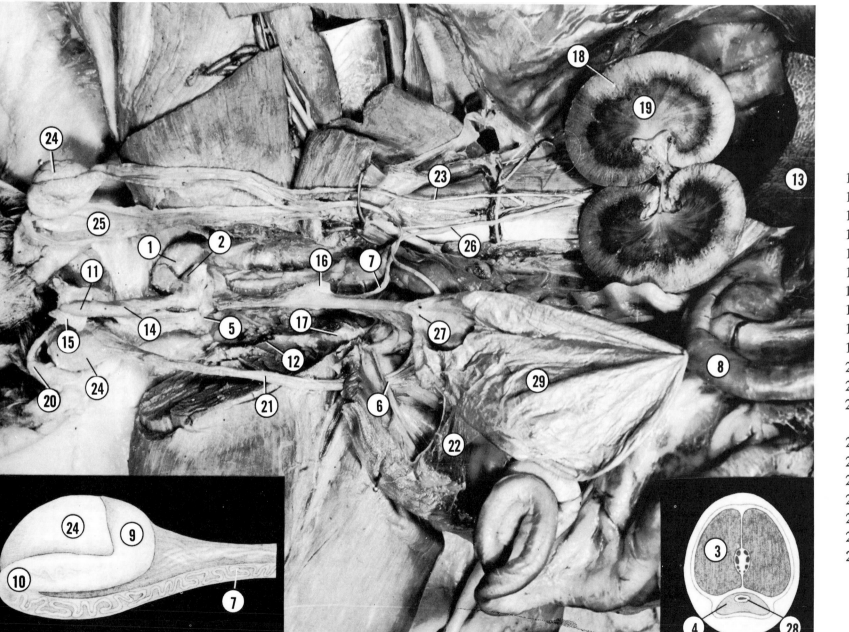

1 anal gland
2 **bulbourethral gland**
3 corpus cavernosum penis
4 corpus spongiosum penis
5 crus of penis
6 **deep inguinal ring**
7 **ductus deferens**
8 duodenum
9 **epididymis, head portion**
10 **epididymis, tail portion**
11 **glans penis**
12 ischium, cut
13 liver
14 **penis**
15 **prepuce**
16 **prostate gland**
17 pubis, cut
18 renal cortex
19 renal medulla
20 **scrotum**
21 **spermatic cord**
22 suspensory ligament of urinary bladder
23 testicular artery and vein
24 **testis**
25 tunica vaginalis, parietal layer
26 **ureter**
27 **ureteral orifice**
28 urethra
29 **urinary bladder**

plate 41

shows both testes dissected from the scrotum, with the right testis displaced laterally to expose the medial side. The left spermatic cord is shown intact, passing through the superficial inguinal ring to enter the inguinal canal, from which the ductus deferens emerges in its mesentery. The right inguinal canal and surrounding muscles have been removed, the right spermatic cord opened, and the ductus deferens and testicular artery and vein separated to show their connecting mesentery. The right kidney has been bisected to show internal structure, with the fat removed from the renal sinus of one half. A window has been cut in the urinary bladder to show the ureteral orifices. In dissecting the pelvis, sections of the ossa coxae have been removed so that the exposed bone can be seen. The penis has been dissected away from the pelvis, with the prepuce cut and turned back to expose the glans penis. One detail inset shows a cross-section of the penis, and the other inset shows a lateral view of the testis.

TESTES

formed retroperitoneally in the same position as the ovaries but, during fetal life, descend through the inguinal canal into the scrotum, preceded by a peritoneal pouch, the processus vaginalis. After the descent of the testes, this peritoneal pouch is called the **tunica vaginalis,** showing the two typical peritoneal layers, the outer **parietal layer,** and the inner **visceral layer** surrounding testis, epididymis, ductus deferens, and blood vessels. The photograph shows the parietal layer opened. Spermatozoa form in the **seminiferous tubules** of the testes, pass through microscopic **efferent ductules** into the **epididymis,** through the **ductus deferens** to the **urethra** at the prostate gland, then to the **external urethral orifice.**

EPIDIDYMIS

epp ih didd′ ih miss. At its **head,** where it is attached to the anterior surface of the testis, the epididymis receives sperm through many microscopic tubules, the **efferent ductules;** it then curves posteriorly as the **body** of the epididymis to the **tail,** which joins the convoluted portion of the **ductus deferens.** The epididymis is derived from the fetal mesonephros.

DUCTUS DEFERENS

duck′ tuss deff′ err ennz—or deferent duct, the fetal mesonephric duct; in adult, conveys only sperm to urethra.

SPERMATIC CORD

an outer membrane of connective tissue, lined by the **parietal layer** of the **tunica vaginalis** and enclosing a very small portion of peritoneal cavity, in which the **testicular artery and vein,** and **ductus deferens** are located. These three structures are usually attached to the parietal layer of the tunica vaginalis by a mesenteric fold running the length of the cord, though in this picture the mesenteric fold has been separated from this parietal layer.

SCROTUM

subcutaneous pouch, partially divided into right and left compartments for the testes.

PROSTATE AND BULBOURETHRAL GLANDS

pross′ tayt, buhl boh iu ree′ thral—contribute to seminal fluid through microscopic ducts to the urethra.

PENIS

pee′ niss—copulatory organ, terminating in a rough **glans penis** surrounded by the **prepuce** (pree′ pius), with the **external urethral orifice** at one side of its tip; composed of two **corpora cavernosa penis** (kor′ poh ruh kavv err noh′ suh), the **corpus spongiosum penis** containing the urethra, and an outer layer of fibrous connective tissue (detail inset). The cavernous bodies contain blood spaces, which may become engorged with blood under pressure and therefore are called **erectile tissues.** The two corpora cavernosa penis diverge at the base of the penis to form the **crura** of the penis, which attach to the ischia along with a muscle, the **ischiocavernosus** muscle.

ANAL GLAND

ay′ nal—part of digestive system, found in cat but not in man; function is uncertain, possibly secretes odoriferous substances aiding sexual attraction.

plate 42 URINARY SYSTEM

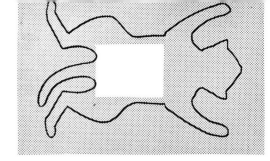

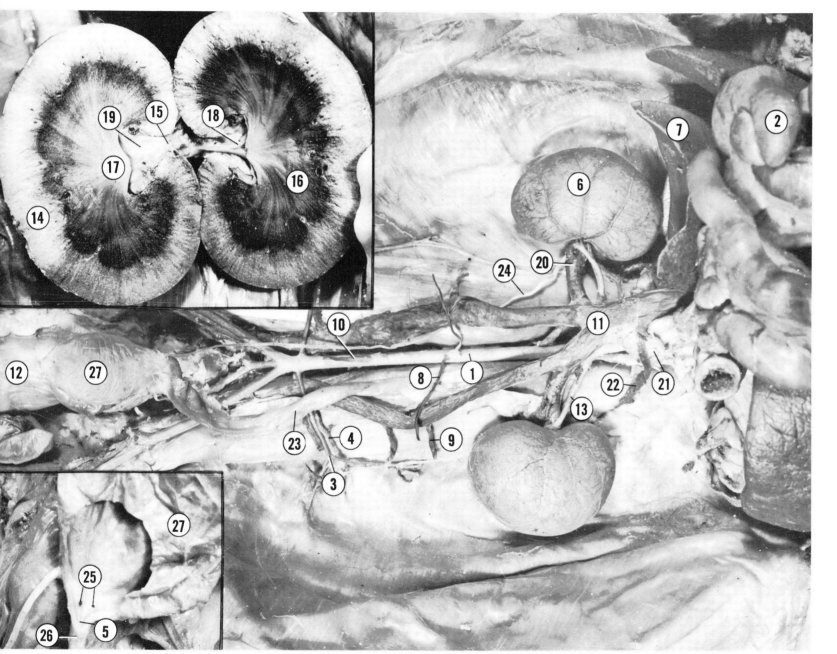

1 abdominal aorta
2 cecum
3 iliolumbar artery
4 iliolumbar vein
5 **internal urethral orifice**
6 **kidney**
7 liver
8 ovarian artery
9 ovarian vein
10 posterior mesenteric artery
11 posterior vena cava
12 rectum
13 renal artery
14 **renal cortex**
15 **renal hilus**
16 **renal medulla**
17 **renal papilla**
18 **renal pelvis**
19 **renal sinus**
20 renal vein
21 suprarenal gland
22 suprarenolumbar vein
23 **ureter, left**
24 **ureter, right**
25 **ureteral orifices**
26 **urethra**
27 **urinary bladder**

plate 42

shows the peritoneum and surrounding fat removed from the kidneys, with the renal capsule also removed from the right kidney. The renal blood vessels and the ureter can be seen at the hilus of each kidney. The right ureter has been dissected free, while the left ureter is still surrounded by fat. This specimen shows a double vena cava (opposite Pl. 50), with the ureters passing atypically medial to the posterior venae cavae to enter the urinary bladder dorsally near its neck. The urinary bladder has been pulled ventrally and posteriorly to show its dorsal side. One detail inset shows a kidney bisected longitudinally through the hilus, dividing the kidney into dorsal and ventral portions, with the ventral half showing the renal sinus freed of fat to expose the ureter and the renal pelvis. The other detail inset shows a window cut in the ventral portion of the urinary bladder to demonstrate the ureteral orifices near the internal urethral orifice forming the trigone.

KIDNEY

dorsal to the peritoneum enclosed in a tough, fibrous renal capsule, which can be removed easily. On the medial surface of the kidney is a dilated area filled with fat, the **renal sinus,** through which the blood vessels and ureter pass, the entrance to which is called the **renal hilus.** The kidney shows an outer **renal cortex** and an inner **renal medulla.** The medullary substance consists of a series of striated conical masses, renal pyramids. Their bases are toward the cortex, while their apices converge toward the renal sinus, where they form renal papillae which project into the lumen of the minor calyces. The minor calyces unite to form short tubes, the major calyces, which in turn join to form a funnel-shaped sac, the renal pelvis, through which the many microscopic renal tubules empty.

URETER

iu ree′ ter—tube which conveys urine from kidney to urinary bladder. Its dilated end, located in the renal sinus, is called the **pelvis,** and its lining is continuous with the surface of the renal medulla at the margin of the pelvis. The ureters are retroperitoneal, lateral to the vena cava until near its posterior end, when they pass ventromediad to the urinary bladder. The ureters enter the urinary bladder obliquely through the wall of the bladder, with the two **ureteral orifices** and the **internal orifice of the urethra** forming a small triangular region, the **trigone** of the bladder.

URINARY BLADDER

supported by the ventral **suspensory ligament** and two **lateral ligaments** usually filled with fat (Pls. 34, 40, 41). The great variations in size of the bladder depend on the volume of urine contained within it (Pls. 40, 41).

URETHRA

iu ree′ thruh—tube from urinary bladder to exterior in the male and to vestibule in the female. In the male it also receives sperm from the right and left ductus deferens as they pass through the prostate gland (Pl. 41).

plate 43   THORACIC CAVITY AND MEDIASTINUM, RIGHT SIDE

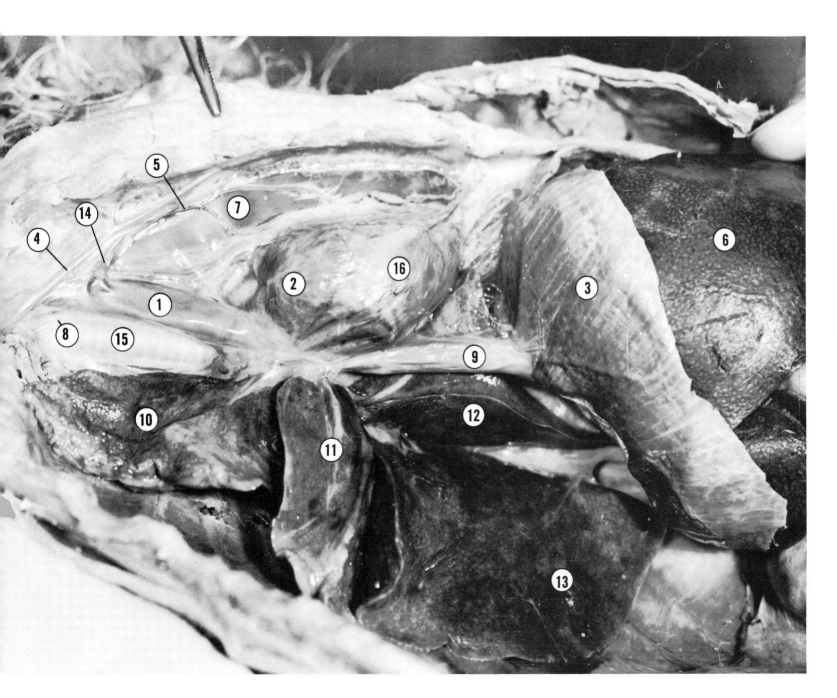

1   anterior vena cava
2   atrium, right
3   **diaphragm**
4   internal thoracic artery
5   internal thoracic vein
6   liver
7   **mediastinum**
8   phrenic nerve
9   posterior vena cava
10 **right lung, first lobe**
11 **right lung, second lobe**
12 **right lung, third lobe**
13 **right lung, fourth lobe**
14 sternal vein
15 trachea
16 ventricle, right

plate 43

shows the thoracic wall cut through the costal cartilages close to the right side of the sternum, to expose the right thoracic cavity and the viscera within it. The ribs have been broken close to the vertebrae, and the diaphragm has been cut along its attachment to the body wall, so that the thoracic wall could be more easily turned back. In order to demonstrate the mediastinum, the sternum has been lifted and pulled to the left.

CELOM

see′ lomm—in mammals is divided into four parts: **abdominal cavity, pericardial cavity,** and two **pleural cavities.**

THORACIC CAVITY

thoh rass′ ick—bounded by the ribs, vertebral column, sternum, and diaphragm. In breathing, the size of the thoracic cavity changes with the movement of the diaphragm, which contracts and pulls posteriorly, and with the movement of the ribs, which rotate and move outward and anteriorly. The thoracic cavity encloses the **pericardial cavity** and the two **pleural cavities.**

DIAPHRAGM

a dome-shaped muscular partition, dividing thoracic cavity from abdominal cavity.

MEDIASTINUM

mee dih ass tai′ numm—a midline partition of connective tissue and pleurae dividing the thoracic cavity into right and left **pleural cavities** and containing all thoracic viscera except the lungs. The thoracic viscera include the trachea, esophagus, thymus gland, and blood vessels. The mediastinum is covered by **parietal pleura** and is filled with connective tissue except at the en-

closure of the pericardial cavity, the pericardium being fused with the mediastinum. In the cat an extra sheet of the mediastinum extends on the right side between the sternum and the posterior vena cava, partially surrounding the third lobe of the right lung.

PLEURAL CAVITIES

lined by two pleurae: **1**—the **parietal pleura,** lining the body wall and covering the mediastinum; **2**—the **visceral pleura,** covering the lungs. Normally the parietal and visceral pleurae are everywhere in contact with each other and are separated by just enough serous pleural fluid to keep the surfaces lubricated.

PERICARDIAL CAVITY

encloses the heart, which is covered by the thin **epicardium** continuous with the serous lining of the pericardium. The pericardium has a layer of connective tissue external to its serous epithelial lining. The **pericardial cavity,** like the abdominal and pleural cavities, contains just enough fluid to keep the surfaces lubricated.

THYMUS GLAND

an endocrine gland located within the anterior portion of the mediastinum. Its size is quite variable, but generally it is larger in the young animal than in the adult. Large thymus glands may extend anteriorly into the neck region and posteriorly to near the diaphragm.

RESPIRATORY SYSTEM

consists of nasal cavities, pharynx, larynx, trachea, and lungs.

NASAL CAVITIES

extend between the **anterior nasal apertures** of the nose and the **posterior nasal apertures,** which open into the

pharynx. These cavities are almost completely filled with **conchae** (kong′ kee), which have a mucosal covering. This increased nasal epithelium is assumed to increase the number of olfactory nerve endings, therefore increasing the efficiency of the olfactory sense as compared with that of man (Pls. 9, 11, and opposite Pl. 9).

PHARYNX

opposite Plate 53.

LARYNX

or voice box; Plate 53.

TRACHEA

tray′ keh uh—conveys air between **larynx** and **bronchi** of lungs and contains rings of cartilage which prevent closure of the passage. The rings are incomplete dorsally, permitting food to pass through the adjacent esophagus.

LUNGS

four lobes on the right side and three lobes on the left. On the right side, the third lobe projects under the posterior vena cava and a special fold of the mediastinum; consequently, it is sometimes called the mediastinal lobe.

HEART

Plate 44.

ANTERIOR VENA CAVA

Plates 45, 46, 47, and opposite Plate 45.

POSTERIOR VENA CAVA

Plates 45, 48, 49, 50, and opposite Plate 50.

plate 44   HEART

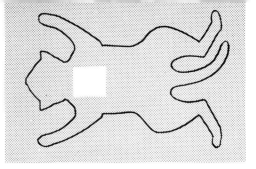

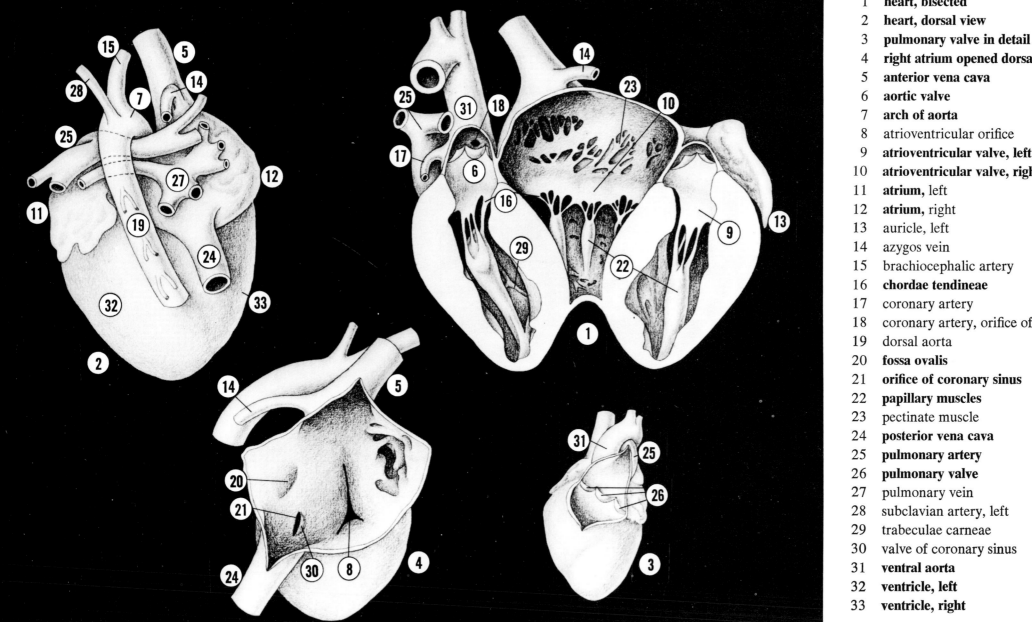

1 **heart, bisected**
2 **heart, dorsal view**
3 **pulmonary valve in detail**
4 **right atrium opened dorsally**
5 **anterior vena cava**
6 **aortic valve**
7 **arch of aorta**
8 atrioventricular orifice
9 **atrioventricular valve, left**
10 **atrioventricular valve, right**
11 **atrium,** left
12 **atrium,** right
13 auricle, left
14 azygos vein
15 brachiocephalic artery
16 **chordae tendineae**
17 coronary artery
18 coronary artery, orifice of
19 dorsal aorta
20 **fossa ovalis**
21 **orifice of coronary sinus**
22 **papillary muscles**
23 pectinate muscle
24 **posterior vena cava**
25 **pulmonary artery**
26 **pulmonary valve**
27 pulmonary vein
28 subclavian artery, left
29 trabeculae carneae
30 valve of coronary sinus
31 **ventral aorta**
32 **ventricle, left**
33 **ventricle, right**

plate 44

shows 4 figures of the heart. Figure 2 is a dorsal view; in Figure 1 the heart has been bisected to demonstrate internal structure, aortic and atrioventricular valves, and the opening of one of the two coronary arteries. In Figure 3 the pulmonary artery has been cut to expose the pulmonary valve, while in Figure 4 the right atrium has been opened between the entrances of the anterior and posterior venae cavae to demonstrate the fossa ovalis and the orifice of the coronary sinus.

CHAMBERS OF HEART

two **atria** and two **ventricles.** The **auricles** are small flaps, which form the ventral part of each atrium. The interiors of the atria, especially in the auricular portion, show irregular bands of muscle, called **pectinate muscles.** The muscular bands in the ventricles are called **trabeculae carneae.** No sinus venosus is present in the cat because it becomes a part of the right atrium during fetal growth.

CIRCULATORY SYSTEM

conveys blood in arteries and veins to and from all parts of the body. It consists of two major divisions: 1—**pulmonary circulation** to lungs and 2—**systemic circulation** to all other capillaries over the body.

COURSE OF BLOOD

In mammals the blood passes through the heart twice in every complete circuit, always from atrium to ventricle. The right atrium receives blood from the body tissues into the systemic veins, viz., anterior and posterior venae cavae and coronary sinus. The sequence from the right atrium is past right atrioventricular valve into right ventricle, past pulmonary valve into pulmonary artery, capillaries of lung, pulmonary veins into left atrium, past left atrioventricular valve into left ventricle, past aortic valve into aorta, systemic capillaries, systemic veins into right atrium again.

AORTIC VALVE

semilunar, with three pockets. It lies flat against the aortic wall as blood leaves the left ventricle but fills with blood as the blood starts to return to the ventricle, thus preventing further backflow. Two of the three pockets cover the entrances of the right and left **coronary arteries,** so that blood enters the coronary arteries only when the ventricles are not contracting.

PULMONARY VALVE

semilunar; functions similarly to the aortic valve.

LEFT ATRIOVENTRICULAR VALVE

of two flat **cusps** of tough connective tissue covered by smooth endocardium. The cusps are held by fine **chordae tendineae** attached to **papillary muscles** in the ventricle, which prevent the cusps from being pushed back into the atrium when it relaxes.

RIGHT ATRIOVENTRICULAR VALVE

structure and function similar to the left, except that it has three cusps.

FOSSA OVALIS

oh vay' liss—thin, slightly depressed area in interatrial septum between right and left atria, formed by the closure of the **foramen ovale,** which permits blood to pass directly from the right to the left atrium during fetal life without going to the lungs through the pulmonary arteries.

CORONARY CIRCULATION

Heart tissue is supplied with blood through the two **coronary arteries,** which branch off the aorta behind two cusps of the aortic valve. The blood returns through small cardiac veins emptying into the coronary sinus, which is found along the atrioventricular groove and enters the right atrium near the orifice of the posterior vena cava. The orifice of the coronary sinus is guarded by a semicircular flap of tissue, called the valve of the coronary sinus.

plate 45 THORACIC BLOOD VESSELS AND NERVES, RIGHT SIDE

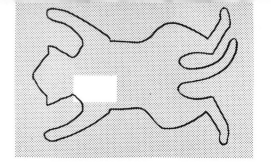

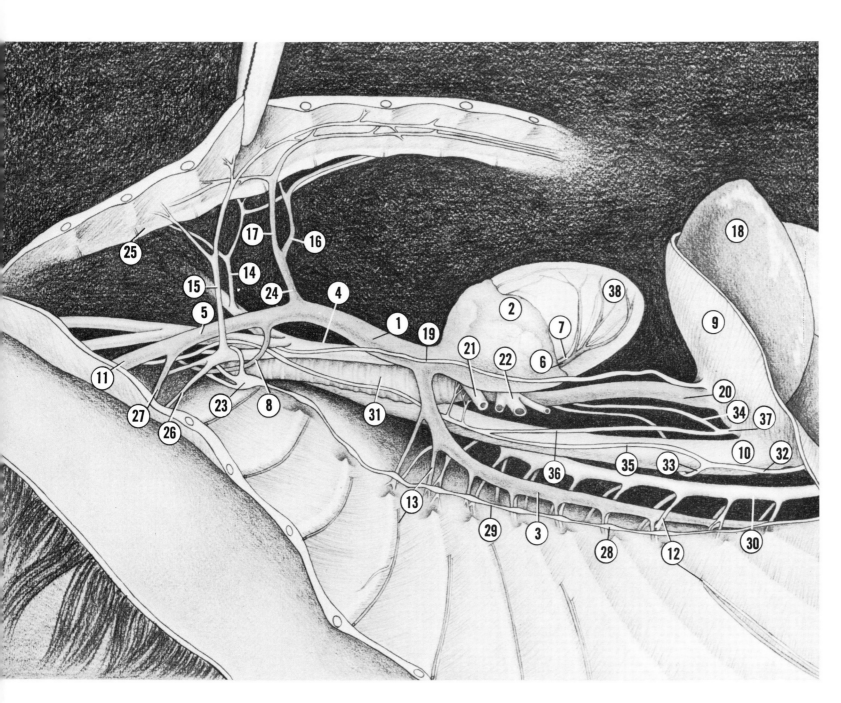

1 **anterior vena cava**
2 auricle of right atrium
3 **azygos vein**
4 brachiocephalic artery
5 brachiocephalic vein
6 cardiac vein
7 coronary artery
8 costocervical and vertebral venous trunk
9 **diaphragm**
10 esophagus
11 external jugular vein
12 intercostal artery
13 intercostal vein
14 **internal thoracic artery, left**
15 **internal thoracic artery, right**
16 **internal thoracic vein, left**
17 **internal thoracic vein, right**
18 liver
19 **phrenic nerve**
20 **posterior vena cava**
21 pulmonary artery
22 pulmonary vein
23 **stellate ganglion**
24 sternal vein
25 sternum
26 subclavian artery
27 subclavian vein
28 sympathetic ganglion
29 sympathetic trunk
30 thoracic aorta
31 trachea
32 **vagus nerve,** dorsal united
33 **vagus nerve,** left dorsal
34 **vagus nerve,** left ventral
35 **vagus nerve,** right dorsal
36 **vagus nerve,** right ventral

plate 45

shows the blood vessels and nerves on the right side of the thoracic cavity. The mediastinum has been dissected away and the pericardium removed to expose the heart. The lungs have been removed, leaving only the larger pulmonary veins and arteries.

ARTERIES

thick-walled and always convey blood away from the heart. Generally they are smaller in diameter than are corresponding veins, and the blood in them is under greater pressure.

VEINS

relatively thin-walled and always carry blood toward the heart.

VARIATIONS IN BLOOD VESSELS

Variations from the so-called "normal" pattern are to be expected, more variations occur in veins than in arteries, and variations in the posterior vena cava caudal to the kidneys occur from specimen to specimen (opposite Pl. 50). A study of the embryology of the blood vessels probably clarifies our understanding of the adult structures more than does the study of embryology of any other system. It is recommended that the student consult a text on embryology.

ANTERIOR VENA CAVA

drains the entire body anterior to the diaphragm, except the lungs, and is formed by the union of the right and left brachiocephalic veins. The **azygos vein** drains the dorsal thoracic wall, while the **sternal vein,** formed from the union of the right and left **internal thoracic veins,** drains the ventral thoracic wall; both join the anterior vena cava (Pls. 46, 47).

POSTERIOR VENA CAVA

drains diaphragm and the body posterior to the diaphragm (Pls. 45, 48, 50, and opposite Pl. 50).

PULMONARY ARTERIES

opposite Plate 47.

PULMONARY VEINS

opposite Plate 47.

AORTA

opposite Plate 47.

INTERNAL THORACIC ARTERIES

supply sternum, mediastinum, and ventral body wall and muscles. They branch from the **subclavian arteries** (opposite Pl. 47).

INTERNAL THORACIC VEINS

from sternum, mediastinum, and ventral body wall. They unite into an unpaired **sternal vein,** which enters the anterior vena cava.

AZYGOS VEIN

azz' ih goss—unpaired, drains dorsal side of the thoracic wall, receives paired **intercostal veins,** and unites with the anterior vena cava on the right side as it enters the right atrium.

37 **vagus nerve,** ventral united
38 ventricle, right

COSTOCERVICAL AND VERTEBRAL VENOUS TRUNK

formed from union of **costocervical** and **vertebral veins** and joins the **brachiocephalic vein** (opposite Pl. 52). The human stellate ganglion results from the fusion of the inferior cervical ganglion and the first thoracic ganglion only. The primary function of the stellate ganglion is in the control of the heart. The fact that the cat stellate ganglion contains more thoracic ganglia may explain differences in clinical observations in experiments with this nervous complex on cats and man.

SYMPATHETIC TRUNK

opposite Plate 46.

STELLATE GANGLION

formed from the union of the **posterior cervical** and **first three thoracic ganglia** (Pls. 46, 51, and opposite Pl. 51).

VAGUS NERVES

opposite Plate 46.

THORACIC DUCT

drains lymphatic vessels into left external jugular vein (opposite Pl. 47).

plate 46 THORACIC BLOOD VESSELS AND NERVES, LEFT SIDE

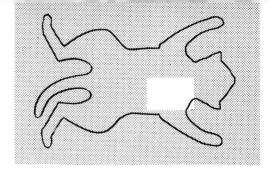

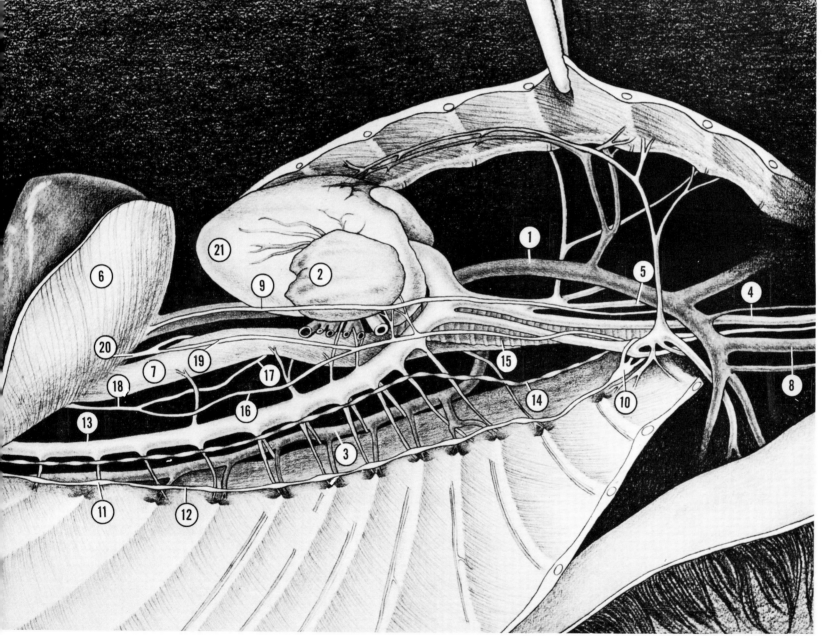

1   anterior vena cava
2   auricle of left atrium
3   azygos vein
4   common carotid artery, left
5   common carotid artery, right
6   diaphragm
7   esophagus
8   external jugular vein
9   **phrenic nerve**
10 **stellate ganglion**
11 **sympathetic ganglion**
12 **sympathetic trunk**
13 thoracic aorta
14 thoracic duct
15 trachea
16 **vagus nerve,** dorsal branch, left
17 **vagus nerve,** dorsal branch, right
18 **vagus nerve,** dorsal united
19 **vagus nerve,** ventral branch, left
20 **vagus nerve,** ventral united
21 ventricle, left

plate 46 shows the blood vessels and nerves in the left side of the thoracic cavity. The mediastinum has been dissected away, the heart freed of pericardium, and the various nerves and blood vessels exposed. The lungs have been removed, leaving only the larger pulmonary veins and arteries.

AUTONOMIC NERVOUS SYSTEM

The physiologists regard this system as an involuntary, functional unit and include all dissectible parts plus such parts of the brain and spinal cord as are used in the autonomic responses, while the anatomists regard it as a visceral efferent subsidiary to the central nervous system and include only the dissectible structures. The autonomic system is distinguished from other motor paths by having two types of motor neurons in sequence: **preganglionic neurons,** with their cell bodies in the lateral columns of the brain and spinal cord, and **postganglionic neurons,** with their cell bodies in autonomic ganglia. One preganglionic neuron stimulates many postganglionic neurons to produce a widespread response. The autonomic system consists of two major parts, often in functional opposition: **1—sympathetic** or **thoracolumbar division,** having preganglionic motor fibers in the thoracic spinal nerves and the first few lumbar nerves (usually the first three or four), and **2— parasympathetic** or **craniosacral division,** having preganglionic motor fibers in cranial nerves (chiefly the oculomotor, facial, glossopharyngeal, vagus, and accessory) and sacral nerves (usually the second, third, and fourth).

SYMPATHETIC NERVOUS SYSTEM

consisting of **1**—two **sympathetic trunks,** extending from anterior cervical ganglion to pelvic region (Pls. 46, 49, 50), and **2—collateral ganglia,** e.g., right and left celiac ganglia, anterior mesenteric ganglion, posterior mesenteric ganglion, and variable small ganglia, often in plexuses without special names in the cat (opposite Pl. 49). Impulses from the central nervous system reach sympathetic ganglia by preganglionic fibers over white communicating branches. Impulses from the ganglia pass over postganglionic fibers either directly to the organs supplied if they lie in the body cavity; or, if they lie in the body wall, e.g., arterioles, indirectly by passing in gray communicating branches to the spinal nerve supplying that region.

PARASYMPATHETIC NERVOUS SYSTEM

consists of **terminal ganglia** which lie either very near, on, or within the organ that they supply. They are so small in the cat as to be impracticable to dissect, e.g., the ciliary ganglion on the oculomotor nerve in the orbit of the eye, cardiac ganglia, and ganglia for the salivary glands. Often these terminal ganglia are minute and in small interconnected groups referred to as plexuses. They send their microscopic postganglionic fibers directly to the organs which they supply.

VISCERAL AFFERENT PATHS

All sensory fibers from sensory end organs in the viscera must pass through the autonomic nerves and ganglia on their way to their cell bodies in the spinal or cranial ganglia; but, since they do not have any synaptic connections in the autonomic ganglia, the sensory impulses must go to the brain or spinal cord before producing motor responses.

VAGUS NERVE

vay′ guss—supplies many viscera with preganglionic autonomic nerve fibers and also carries afferent nerve fibers. This nerve leaves the skull through the jugular foramen, passes with the cervical sympathetic trunk beside the common carotid artery to the middle cervical ganglion, where it turns ventrally (Pls. 45, 51). Very small nerves branch from the vagus nerve to the heart, lungs, larynx, esophagus, and large arteries. Each vagus nerve divides into a ventral and a dorsal branch in the region of the heart and lungs, the division point showing considerable variation. The right and left ventral branches unite into a single ventral branch, which is located on the ventral surface of the esophagus, while the right and left dorsal branches unite into a single dorsal branch on the dorsal side of the esophagus. Usually the dorsal branches unite a short distance anterior to the diaphragm, while the ventral branches unite more anteriorly (Pl. 45). Both united branches pass through the diaphragm to ramify on the stomach, the ventral branch on the lesser curvature and the dorsal branch on the greater curvature. Branches of the vagus nerve supply other viscera, but are too small to be seen in dissection of the cat.

plate 47 THORACIC BLOOD VESSELS AND NERVES, LEFT SIDE

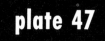

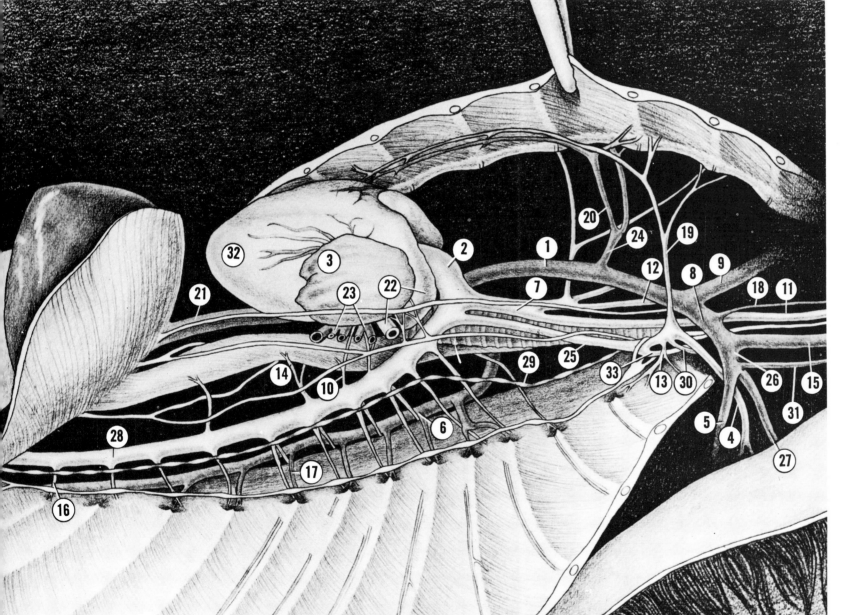

1 **anterior vena cava**
2 **arch of aorta**
3 **auricle** of **left atrium**
4 **axillary artery**
5 axillary vein
6 **azygos vein**
7 **brachiocephalic artery**
8 **brachiocephalic vein,** left
9 **brachiocephalic vein,** right
10 bronchial artery
11 **common carotid artery,** left
12 common carotid artery, right
13 **costocervical trunk**
14 esophageal artery
15 **external jugular vein**
16 intercostal artery
17 intercostal vein
18 **internal jugular vein**
19 **internal thoracic artery**
20 **internal thoracic vein,** left
21 **posterior vena cava**
22 **pulmonary artery**
23 **pulmonary veins**
24 **sternal vein**
25 **subclavian artery,** left
26 **subclavian vein**
27 subscapular vein
28 **thoracic aorta**
29 **thoracic duct**
30 thyrocervical arterial trunk
31 thyrocervical venous trunk
32 ventricle, left
33 vertebral artery

plate 47

shows the blood vessels and nerves in the left side of the thoracic cavity. The mediastinum has been dissected away, the heart freed of pericardium, and the various nerves and blood vessels exposed. The lungs have been removed, leaving only the larger pulmonary veins and arteries.

AORTA

ay orr' tuh—large artery from the left ventricle. Called **ventral aorta** as it leaves the ventricle, **arch of the aorta** as it turns dorsally, **dorsal aorta** as it continues posteriorly. These terms are derived from the embryonic condition in which there are several aortic arches connecting the ventral and the dorsal aortae; the left fourth aortic arch is the one remaining as a part of the adult aorta. The dorsal aorta has two regions, **thoracic aorta** and **abdominal aorta.**

PULMONARY ARTERY

from the right ventricle to the lungs. It divides immediately into right and left pulmonary arteries and then into branches for each lobe of a lung.

PULMONARY VEINS

from lungs to left atrium; very short. Typically there are three pulmonary veins formed by the union of smaller veins just before they enter the left atrium.

BRACHIOCEPHALIC ARTERY

gives off the **right subclavian artery** and divides into the right and left **common carotid arteries.** It was the ventral aorta in the embryo but now appears to come from the arch of the aorta.

SUBCLAVIAN ARTERIES

are asymmetrical because of their embryological origin. For branches of each see opposite Plate 52.

ANTERIOR VENA CAVA

opposite Plate 45.

BRACHIOCEPHALIC VEINS

opposite Plate 52.

AZYGOS VEIN

opposite Plate 45.

LYMPHATIC VESSELS

The smallest vessels are called **lymphatic capillaries.** These drain into progressively larger lymphatic vessels until they reach either the **thoracic duct,** which empties into the left external jugular vein, or the **right lymphatic duct,** which empties into the right external jugular vein. The exact point of entrance of the lymphatics into the veins is extremely variable. They may empty into the subclavian vein or by several channels. The lymphatic vessels either appear similar to veins and are not readily distinguishable during dissection, or, in the larger lymphatics that are distended or injected, they have a beaded appearance due to distention between valves. The valves are semilunar in form and similar to those at the base of the aorta and pulmonary artery.

LYMPH

is contained in the lymphatic vessels and probably filters and diffuses from the surrounding tissue fluid into the lymphatic capillaries. Part of the tissue fluid is a product of cell metabolism, but most of it is derived from filtration of the smaller molecules of blood plasma through the thin blood capillary walls. Fundamentally, lymph is derived from blood and is returned to the blood stream through the veins of the neck.

THORACIC DUCT

lymphatic vessel, draining all the lymphatics except the right head, neck, and shoulder vessels. It empties into the left external jugular vein.

LYMPH NODES

or lymph glands, are masses of lymphoid tissue interposed as filters on lymphatic vessels in various parts of the body (Pls. 20, 51). They help to prevent bacteria from getting into the blood stream and also serve as a place for the production of the nongranular white corpuscles.

plate 48

ABDOMINAL BLOOD VESSELS AND NERVES, RIGHT SIDE

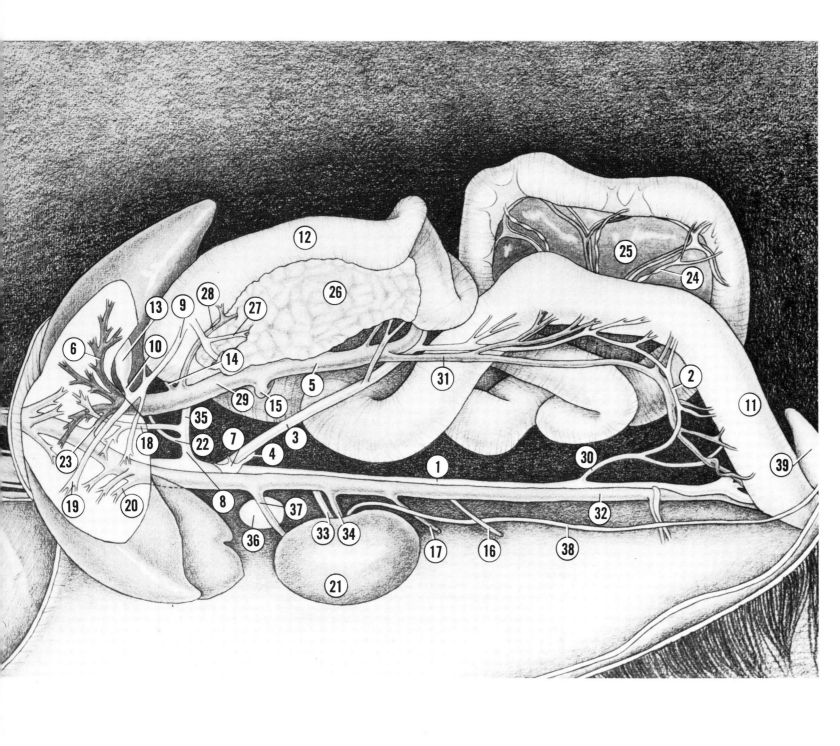

1 abdominal aorta
2 **anastomosis of anterior and posterior mesenteric arteries**
3 anterior mesenteric artery
4 anterior mesenteric ganglion
5 **anterior mesenteric vein**
6 **branch of portal vein**
7 celiac ganglion
8 celiac trunk
9 **common bile duct**
10 cystic duct
11 descending colon
12 duodenum
13 gall bladder
14 gastroepiploic vein
15 gastrolienal vein
16 gonadal artery, cut
17 gonadal vein, cut
18 **hepatic artery**
19 **hepatic duct**
20 **hepatic vein**
21 kidney
22 left gastric artery
23 **ligamentum venosum**
24 **lymphatic vessel**
25 **mesentery proper**
26 pancreas, right lobe
27 **pancreatic duct**
28 pancreatoduodenal vein
29 **portal vein**
30 posterior mesenteric artery
31 **posterior mesenteric vein**
32 **posterior vena cava**
33 renal artery
34 renal vein
35 splenic artery

plate 48

shows the arteries and veins on the right side of the abdominal cavity dissected free of connective tissue and fat. The liver is drawn with a part cut away, in order to show a diagram of the circulation through the liver and the plan of the hepatic, bile, and cystic ducts. The pancreatic duct has been exposed by removal of some of the pancreatic tissue.

PORTAL SYSTEM

veins which drain the stomach, intestines, and spleen and unite into the **portal vein,** which branches repeatedly, eventually emptying into special capillaries in the liver called **hepatic sinusoids.** The veins forming the portal vein are **1—posterior mesenteric vein,** draining colon and emptying into anterior mesenteric vein; **2—anterior mesenteric vein,** receiving blood from intestines; **3—gastrolienal vein,** receiving blood from a—gastric part of pancreas, b—stomach and spleen, c—posterior end of spleen.

HEPATIC ARTERY

supplies oxygenated blood to the hepatic sinusoids, where it is mixed with the blood from the portal vein. The digestive system and spleen absorb the available oxygen from the blood before it reaches the portal vein, making necessary an arterial supply to the liver.

HEPATIC VEINS

drain blood from the sinusoids of the liver into the posterior vena cava. The liver keeps the sugar content of the blood relatively constant by absorbing excess sugar in the blood as it comes from the digestive system or by adding sugar to it if the sugar level is low. The liver also deaminizes some excess amino acids, forming urea and sugar, and subjects the portal blood to various other metabolic processes.

POSTERIOR VENA CAVA

opposite Plate 50.

CELIAC TRUNK

opposite Plate 49.

ANTERIOR MESENTERIC ARTERY

opposite Plate 49.

LIGAMENTUM VENOSUM

fibrous cord connecting one branch of the portal vein with the posterior vena cava. It is the remains of the fetal **ductus venosus,** which passes blood from the umbilical vein directly through the liver to the posterior vena cava.

36 suprarenal gland
37 suprarenolumbar vein
38 ureter
39 urinary bladder

COMMON BILE DUCT

The liver secretes bile into small **hepatic ducts,** which empty into the **common bile duct,** which, in turn, empties into the duodenum at the **duodenal papilla.**

CYSTIC DUCT

receives excess bile, carries it to the gall bladder, where it is stored (Pl. 33).

PANCREATIC DUCT

short, formed from right and left branches draining the lobes of the pancreas. It empties into the common bile duct within the duodenal wall, where both pancreatic duct and common bile duct empty through a common orifice on the duodenal papilla.

plate 49

ABDOMINAL BLOOD VESSELS AND NERVES, LEFT SIDE

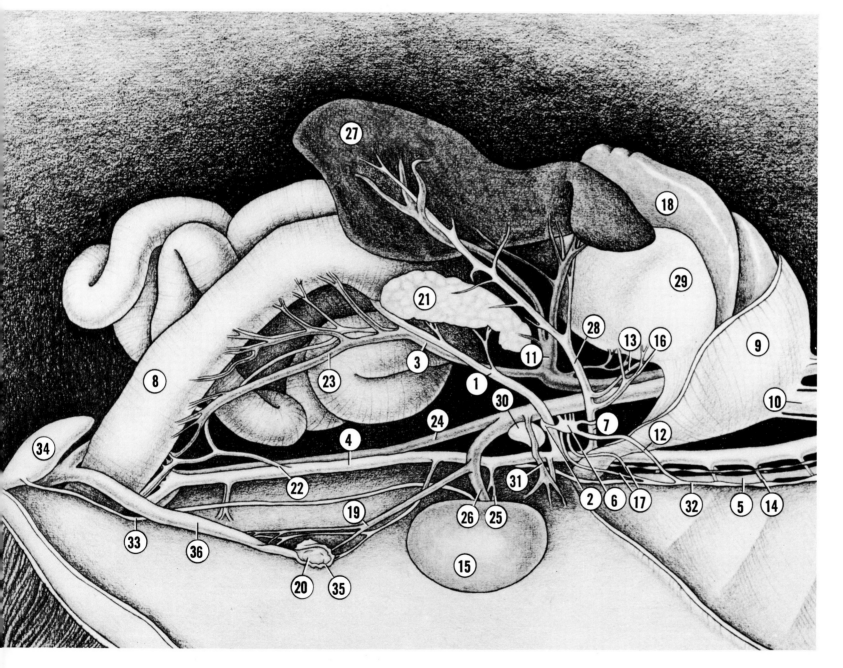

1   **anterior mesenteric artery**
2   **anterior mesenteric ganglion**
3   **anterior mesenteric vein**
4   aorta
5   azygos vein
6   **celiac ganglion**
7   **celiac trunk**
8   descending colon
9   diaphragm
10 esophagus
11 gastrolienal vein
12 **greater splanchnic nerve**
13 hepatic artery
14 intercostal artery
15 kidney
16 left gastric artery
17 **lesser splanchnic nerves**
18 liver
19 ovarian vein
20 ovary
21 pancreas, left lobe
22 **posterior mesenteric artery**
23 posterior mesenteric vein
24 posterior vena cava
25 renal artery
26 renal vein
27 spleen
28 splenic artery
29 stomach
30 **suprarenal gland**
31 suprarenolumbar vein
32 **sympathetic trunk**
33 ureter
34 urinary bladder
35 uterine tube
36 uterus, left horn

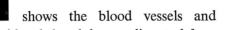

shows the blood vessels and nerves on the left side of the abdomen dissected free. The large intestine has been raised to demonstrate the mesenteric vessels, and the spleen has been displaced toward the right side of the cat.

CELIAC TRUNK

see' lih ack—unpaired, divides into **1—hepatic artery,** to liver with several small branches to stomach, duodenum, and pancreas; **2—left gastric artery,** to stomach on left side; **3—splenic artery,** largest branch, appearing as a continuation of the celiac.

ANTERIOR MESENTERIC ARTERY

supplies small intestine with many branches.

POSTERIOR MESENTERIC ARTERY

divides into anterior and posterior branches to supply large intestine. Usually has an **anastomosis** with a branch of the anterior mesenteric artery.

ANASTOMOSIS

uh nass toh moh' sis—a union of one blood vessel with another of the same type, artery with artery and vein with vein. Anastomoses are fairly common. If the normal circulatory path is in any way interrupted, anastomosing vessels help to keep the part supplied, and the anastomosis often enlarges (Pl. 48).

COLLATERAL GANGLIA

part of the sympathetic nervous system (opposite Pl. 46). Those located in the abdominal area are the **right and left celiac ganglion,** the **anterior mesenteric ganglion,** and the **posterior mesenteric ganglion.** The **right celiac ganglion** is shown in Plate 48. Other collateral ganglia doubtless exist in the cat but are too small to be observed in dissection.

CELIAC PLEXUS

or solar plexus, consists of right and left **celiac ganglia** lateral to the anterior mesenteric artery, the unpaired **anterior mesenteric ganglion** posterior to the anterior mesenteric artery, and a network of nerves. These ganglia may be so close together as to fuse into one mass, or they may be quite separate. The celiac ganglia are connected to the sympathetic trunk by the splanchnic nerves.

SPLANCHNIC NERVES

connect **thoracic sympathetic trunks** and the **celiac ganglia.** The **greater splanchnic nerves** passing through the diaphragm are easily found, but the **lesser splanchnic nerves** are small, variable in number, and difficult to dissect.

POSTERIOR MESENTERIC PLEXUS

consists of a network of nerves and usually one small **posterior mesenteric ganglion,** though sometimes two, a right and a left ganglion, are found, located beside the posterior mesenteric artery about ¼–½ inch distal to the origin of the artery from the aorta. The posterior mesenteric plexus is connected to the celiac plexus by small nerves in the mesentery.

SUPRARENAL GLANDS

or **adrenal glands,** in the cat are located near the base of the celiac artery and celiac ganglia, not as close to the kidney as in man. They are important endocrine glands.

SYMPATHETIC TRUNK

Plates 45, 46, 50, and opposite Plate 46.

ABDOMINAL AORTA

opposite Plate 50.

POSTERIOR VENA CAVA

opposite Plate 50.

plate 50   ABDOMINAL BLOOD VESSELS, VISCERA REMOVED, VENTRAL VIEW

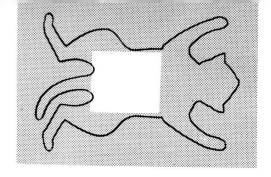

1   **abdominal aorta**
2   anterior gluteal artery
3   anterior gluteal vein
4   anterior mesenteric artery
5   **common iliac vein**
6   deep femoral artery
7   deep femoral vein
8   **external iliac artery**
9   **external iliac vein**
10   femoral artery
11   femoral vein
12   **gonadal artery**
13   **gonadal vein**
14   hepatic artery
15   hepatic vein
16   **iliolumbar artery**
17   **iliolumbar vein**
18   iliopsoas muscle
19   **internal iliac artery**
20   **internal iliac vein**
21   kidney
22   liver
23   lumbar artery and vein
24   middle rectal artery
25   middle rectal vein
26   middle sacral artery
27   muscular artery
28   muscular vein
29   phrenic artery
30   posterior epigastric artery
31   posterior epigastric vein
32   posterior gluteal artery
33   posterior gluteal vein
34   posterior mesenteric artery
35   **posterior vena cava**
36   rectum, cut

plate 50

shows the arteries, veins, and nerves of the abdominal region after the removal of most of the viscera. The stomach, liver, and diaphragm have been pulled anteriorly. The gonadal veins, here ovarian, have been cut and displaced laterally, while the gonadal arteries were cut and laid at right angles to the aorta to avoid confusion with other structures. Both the posterior vena cava and the aorta have been pulled to the right of the specimen to expose the underlying sympathetic nerve trunks and the lumbar arteries and veins which would normally pass directly dorsally. The rectum has been cut and its end, along with the urinary bladder, uterus, and vagina, pulled posteriorly into the pelvic area, previously opened by a cut through the ischiopubic symphysis.

ABDOMINAL AORTA

branches into arteries of three types. **1**—Unpaired, median, supply viscera: **celiac trunk, anterior mesenteric,** and **posterior mesenteric arteries. 2**—Paired, supply urogenital system which is embryologically ventrolateral: **renal, ovarian,** or **testicular arteries. 3**—Paired, supply body wall: **lumbar, suprarenolumbar, iliolumbar, external iliac,** and **internal iliac arteries.**

EXTERNAL ILIAC ARTERY

bifurcates as it emerges from the celom into two branches. **1**—**Deep femoral artery,** which then divides into three branches: **a**—**vesicular artery** supplying the bladder; **b**—**superficial epigastric artery** to the skin on the medial surface of the thigh and to the external genitalia; and **c**—**posterior epigastric artery,** which supplies the rectus abdominis muscle and anastomoses with the internal thoracic artery on the ventral abdominal wall. **2**—**Femoral artery,** which courses down the medial

surface of the thigh and gives off several branches: **a**—**lateral circumflex femoral** to the muscles of the front of the thigh, rectus femoris, vastus medialis, sartorius, tensor fascia lata muscles and the hip joint; **b**—a large **muscular artery** to the adductor femoris and gracilis muscles; and **c**—**anterior (superior) articular artery** to the medial surface of the knee between the vastus medialis and semimembranous muscles. The **femoral artery** then divides into the **d**—**saphenous artery,** which is superficial to shank and foot, and **e**—**popliteal artery,** which becomes deep and supplies the calf of the leg.

INTERNAL ILIAC ARTERY

or **hypogastric artery,** has several branches. **1**—**Umbilical artery,** supplies the bladder; in this picture it is pulled out longer than is its normal length. **2**—**Anterior gluteal artery,** supplies pelvic muscles. **3**—**Middle rectal artery,** supplies rectum, vagina, or prostate gland, and anal structures. **4**—**Posterior gluteal artery,** accompanies sciatic nerve to supply thigh muscles.

POSTERIOR VENA CAVA

vee' nuh kay' vuh—formed by the union of the two **common iliac veins,** normally is located on the right side of the cat and receives **lumbar, iliolumbar, gonadal,** and **renal veins.** Between the kidneys it is asymmetric because of its embryological origin. On the right side it is joined by the **right gonadal, renal,** and **suprarenolumbar veins** separately, while on the left side the renal vein receives the **left gonadal** and **left suprarenolumbar veins** before uniting with the vena cava. Variation is very common in the posterior vena cava and its tributaries, since the embryological pattern develops one set of vessels and later reorganizes to replace it with other vessels. Any embryology or comparative anat-

omy text may be referred to for details. Common examples are double posterior venae cavae either connected with each other or unconnected, or a left instead of a right posterior vena cava. Frequently the renal arteries and veins are double, and also occasionally there may be three connected with one kidney. The veins, in general, follow the pattern of the arteries.

ABDOMINAL NERVES

either are derived from spinal nerves or are branches of the autonomic system (opposite Pl. 46). The spinal nerves are not shown here. The **sympathetic trunks** lie on either side of the lumbar arteries and lumbar veins, quite close to the bodies of the lumbar vertebrae. Branches to the viscera have been removed in this dissection, along with the small nerves of the sacral plexus.

37	**renal artery**
38	**renal vein**
39	superficial epigastric artery
40	superficial epigastric vein
41	**suprarenolumbar artery**
42	**suprarenolumbar vein**
43	**sympathetic ganglion**
44	**sympathetic trunk**
45	tendon of psoas minor muscle
46	umbilical artery
47	ureter, cut
48	urinary bladder
49	uterus

plate 51   GLANDS AND NERVES OF NECK, LEFT SIDE

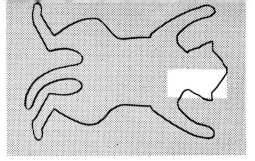

1 **anterior cervical ganglion**
2 anterior vena cava
3 **cervical sympathetic trunk**
4 common carotid artery, left
5 common carotid artery, right
6 internal jugular vein
7 larynx
8 lymph node
9 masseter muscle
10 **middle cervical ganglion**
11 **parathyroid gland**
12 **parotid duct**
13 **parotid gland**
14 **phrenic nerve**
15 **posterior ganglion of vagus nerve**
16 **stellate ganglion**
17 subclavian artery
18 **sublingual gland**
19 **submandibular gland**
20 **submandibular** and **sublingual ducts**
21 **thyroid gland,** left lobe
22 trachea
23 **vagus nerve**

plate 51

shows the neck dissected on the left side to show nerves, blood vessels, and salivary glands. The left detail inset shows the stellate and middle cervical ganglia, and the right inset shows the posterior ganglion of the vagus nerve and the anterior cervical ganglion of the cervical sympathetic trunk. The blood vessels and lymph nodes have been pulled laterally to expose the sublingual gland and the submandibular duct. The left parathyroid gland can be seen on the dorsal side of the left lobe of the thyroid gland, which has been turned to the right.

SALIVARY GLANDS

secrete saliva into mouth for lubrication and perhaps for aiding digestion. Man has three pairs: the **submandibular, sublingual,** and **parotid.** The cat has, in addition, small **molar glands** on each side under the skin near the lower lip and **infraorbital glands** in the orbit ventrolateral to the eye.

SUBMANDIBULAR GLAND

lies deep to two lymph nodes near the angle of the mandible. Its surface appears to be more smooth and less subdivided than that of similar structures. The **submandibular duct** lies parallel to the sublingual duct and opens through a papilla onto the floor of the mouth near the midline just anterior to the tongue.

SUBLINGUAL GLAND

very small and appears to be a pointed continuation of the submandibular gland along the submandibular duct. The **sublingual duct** parallels the submandibular duct and enters the mouth with it.

PAROTID GLAND

puh rott' idd—largest of the group of salivary glands and found just beneath the skin ventral to the external acoustic meatus. Its duct lies just under the skin, embedded within the fascia of the masseter muscle, and opens into the mouth between the largest cusp of the last premolar tooth and the cheek of the upper jaw.

THYROID GLAND

usually consists of separate right and left lobes in the cat, though in some specimens these are connected ventrally by a narrow isthmus across the trachea.

PARATHYROID GLANDS

located on the dorsal side of the thyroid gland near its anterior end and are usually lighter in color than the thyroid gland.

CERVICAL GANGLIA

The sympathetic ganglia in the neck region consists of the **anterior cervical ganglion,** the small **middle cervical ganglion,** and the **posterior cervical ganglion** which is fused with the first three thoracic ganglia to form the **stellate ganglion.** These cervical ganglia are united by the cervical portion of the sympathetic trunk. The middle cervical ganglion may be absent or too small to be detected in some cats; it is usually found on the cervical sympathetic trunk near the junction of the vagus nerve and sympathetic trunk. The middle cervical ganglion is connected to the stellate ganglion by two nerves, one of which passes over, and one under, the subclavian artery (inset). In the neck the vagus nerve and cervical sympathetic trunk are held together by connective tissue and appear to be one nerve until dissected apart. They are also usually bound with the common carotid artery in a connective-tissue sheath.

PHRENIC NERVE

frenn' ick—supplies the diaphragm. This nerve is formed from branches of the fifth and sixth cervical nerves and passes on the surface of the mediastinum near the venae cavae to the diaphragm (Pls. 45, 46). It lies near the vagus nerve and cervical sympathetic trunk but is in no way connected with the autonomic nervous system.

plate 52

BLOOD VESSELS OF NECK, LEFT SIDE

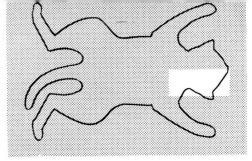

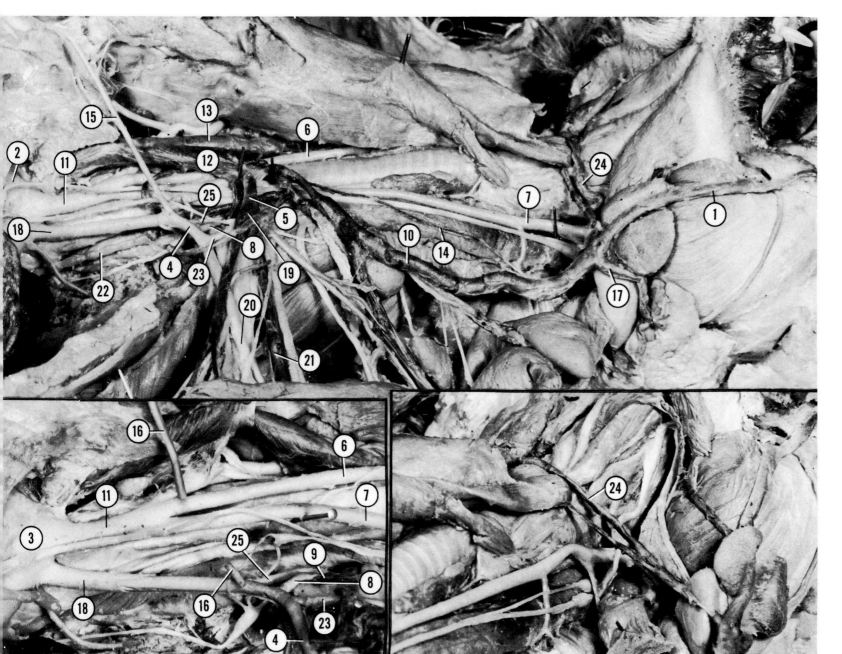

1 facial vein
2 **aorta, ventral portion**
3 **arch of aorta**
4 **axillary artery**
5 **subclavian vein**
6 **common carotid artery, right**
7 **common carotid artery, left**
8 costocervical trunk
9 costocervical vein
10 **external jugular vein**
11 **brachiocephalic artery**
12 **brachiocephalic vein, left**
13 **brachiocephalic vein, right**
14 **internal jugular vein**
15 internal thoracic artery
16 internal thoracic artery, cut
17 communication between facial and external jugular veins
18 **subclavian artery**
19 **axillary vein**
20 subscapular artery
21 subscapular vein
22 **thoracic duct**
23 thyrocervical trunk
24 transverse vein
25 vertebral artery

plate 52

shows the neck dissected on the left side to exhibit blood vessels, nerves, and salivary glands. One detail inset shows the stellate and middle cervical ganglia, while a second inset shows the posterior ganglion of the vagus nerve and the anterior cervical ganglion of the cervical sympathetic trunk. The blood vessels and lymph nodes have been pulled laterally to expose the sublingual gland and the submandibular duct. The left parathyroid gland can be seen on the dorsal side of the left lobe of the thyroid gland, which has been turned to the right.

SUBCLAVIAN ARTERY

subb klay' vih ann—supplies arm and shoulder regions. Its principal branches are **1—vertebral artery,** passing deep into the neck to enter the transverse foramina of cervical vertebrae to supply the brain; **2—internal thoracic artery,** to sternum, mediastinum and thorax; **3—costocervical trunk,** to first two intercostal spaces and serratus anterior, levator scapulae, and rhomboid muscles; **4—thyrocervical trunk,** a large artery with numerous branches to neck region, including branches to the trapezius, subscapularis, and supraspinatus muscles. Lateral to these branches the artery is called the **axillary artery** (ack' sih lerr ih; ack sill' uh rih). The axillary artery gives off **1**— the small **anterior thoracic artery** to the medial ends of the pectoral muscles (Pl. 19) and **2**—the **lateral thoracic artery** to the middle portions of the pectoral muscles and the deep surface of the latissimus dorsi. The axillary artery then divides into **1—subscapular artery,** anteriorly, which supplies numerous muscles, including the latissimus dorsi, long head of triceps brachii, subscapularis, supraspinatus, acromiotrapezius, and spinotrapezius; **2—brachial artery,** posteriorly, supplying arm. It passes on the humeral side of the biceps brachii muscle.

COMMON CAROTID ARTERY

kuh rott' idd—supplies head and neck. Gives off several small branches and divides near the skull into the small **internal carotid artery** to the brain and the larger **external carotid artery** with numerous branches to the face.

BRACHIOCEPHALIC VEIN

formed by the union of the **subclavian** and **external jugular veins.** It also receives a short trunk formed by the union of the **vertebral** and **costocervical veins.** Variations are common.

EXTERNAL JUGULAR VEIN

jugg' iu lerr—formed by the union of the posterior division of the retromandibular and the posterior auricular veins, and drains the greater part of the exterior of the cranium and the deep parts of the face. It has several tributaries: **1—suprascapular vein,** from region anterior to scapula; **2—transverse cervical vein,** from muscles of neck; **3—internal jugular vein,** from head and located very close to the vagus and cervical sympathetic nerves and the carotid artery. The internal jugular vein is extremely variable in size and may even be absent, or may enter the brachiocephalic vein instead of the external jugular (Pl. 47). The **thoracic duct** of the lymphatic vessels enters the external jugular vein near its junction with the subclavian vein.

SUBCLAVIAN VEIN

very short and is called the **axillary vein** at the border of the first rib. The axillary vein receives the large **subscapular vein** with the **brachial vein** from the arm. The subscapular vein is the more anterior of the two. The axillary vein also receives the small **anterior thoracic vein** from the medial ends of the pectoral muscles and the **lateral thoracic vein** from the middle portions of the pectoral muscles and the latissimus dorsi muscle.

LYMPH NODES

masses of lymphoid tissue (opposite Pl. 47).

plate 53   MOUTH, PHARYNX, AND LARYNX

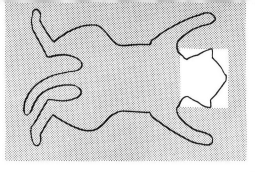

1   anterior cervical ganglion
2   aryepiglottic fold
3   cervical sympathetic trunk
4   common carotid artery
5   **epiglottis**
6   esophagus
7   external carotid artery
8   **glottis**
9   **hard palate**
10 **laryngopharynx**
11 **larynx**
12 **nasopharynx**
13 **opening of auditory tube,** right
14 orifice of parotid duct
15 **oropharynx**
16 **palatine tonsil**
17 posterior ganglion of vagus nerve
18 **soft palate**
19 tongue
20 trachea
21 vagus nerve
22 ventricular fold
23 **vocal fold**

plate 53

shows the mouth and esophagus opened on the left side to expose the structures of the throat. The larynx has been turned to the right, so that a dorsal view of the glottis and epiglottis has been obtained. The detail inset shows the larynx and trachea cut mid-dorsally to expose the vocal folds, and the soft palate cut away to show the opening of the right auditory tube.

PHARYNX

far′ inks—common passageway for digestive and respiratory systems. The soft palate partially separates the nasal part of the pharynx from the mouth. The mouth, esophagus, choanae, glottis, and auditory tubes open into the pharynx. Food passes from the mouth dorsally to the esophagus, while air crosses this path and passes ventrally between the choanae and the glottis. The epiglottis covers the glottis during swallowing, so that food cannot enter the air passage. The pharynx in the cat has three parts, named according to location: **nasopharynx, oropharynx, laryngopharynx.**

TONSILS

The **palatine tonsils** are located on the dorsal side of the soft palate. In the cat, only a small part of the tonsil protrudes from the palate into the pharynx. Most of the mass of the tonsil is embedded behind the palate, as demonstrated in the photograph. In man there is also a pharyngeal tonsil present on the dorsal side of the nasopharynx, and when enlarged it is called the adenoids. Such an enlarged condition often occurs in cats as a reddish, soft mass on the posterior surface of the nasopharynx between the orifices of the auditory tubes. Tonsils are composed of lymphoid tissue.

AUDITORY TUBES

from middle ear to nasal part of pharynx. These tubes enable air to enter the middle ears, so that the air pressure is the same on both inner and outer surfaces of the tympanic membrane.

PALATE

roof of mouth; in two parts: **hard palate** and **soft palate.** The hard palate is supported by the premaxillae, maxillae, and palatine bones (Pls. 6 and 11) and is marked by conspicuous transverse ridges on its surface. The soft palate is smooth, unsupported by bone, and separates the mouth cavity from the nasopharynx.

TONGUE

in the cat has many pointed **filiform papillae.** Those on the central area of the tongue are covered with a very hard corneal layer, are directed posteriorly, and can be used for scraping. There are also a few **fungiform papillae,** variably located at the sides and back of the tongue.

LARYNX

lar′ inks—or voice box, between glottis and trachea. It contains the vocal folds.

VOCAL FOLDS

folds of membrane on either side of the glottis, which are put under varying degrees of tension by movement of the cartilages in the wall of the larynx. Air currents cause these taut folds to vibrate, thus producing sound, which is modified by the position of the mouth. The function of the ventricular folds or false vocal folds is uncertain.

plate 54   BRAIN AND SPINAL CORD, DORSAL VIEW

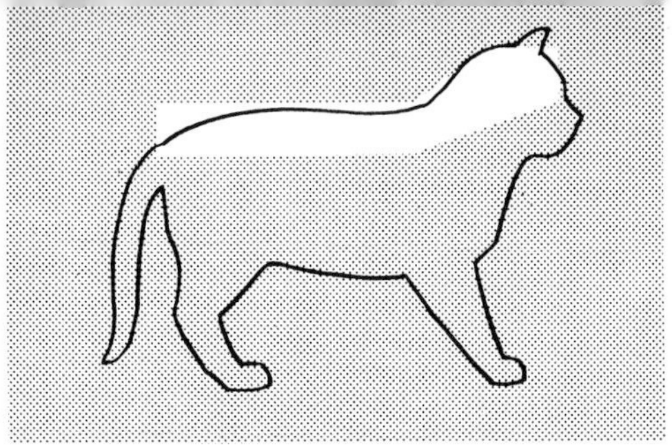

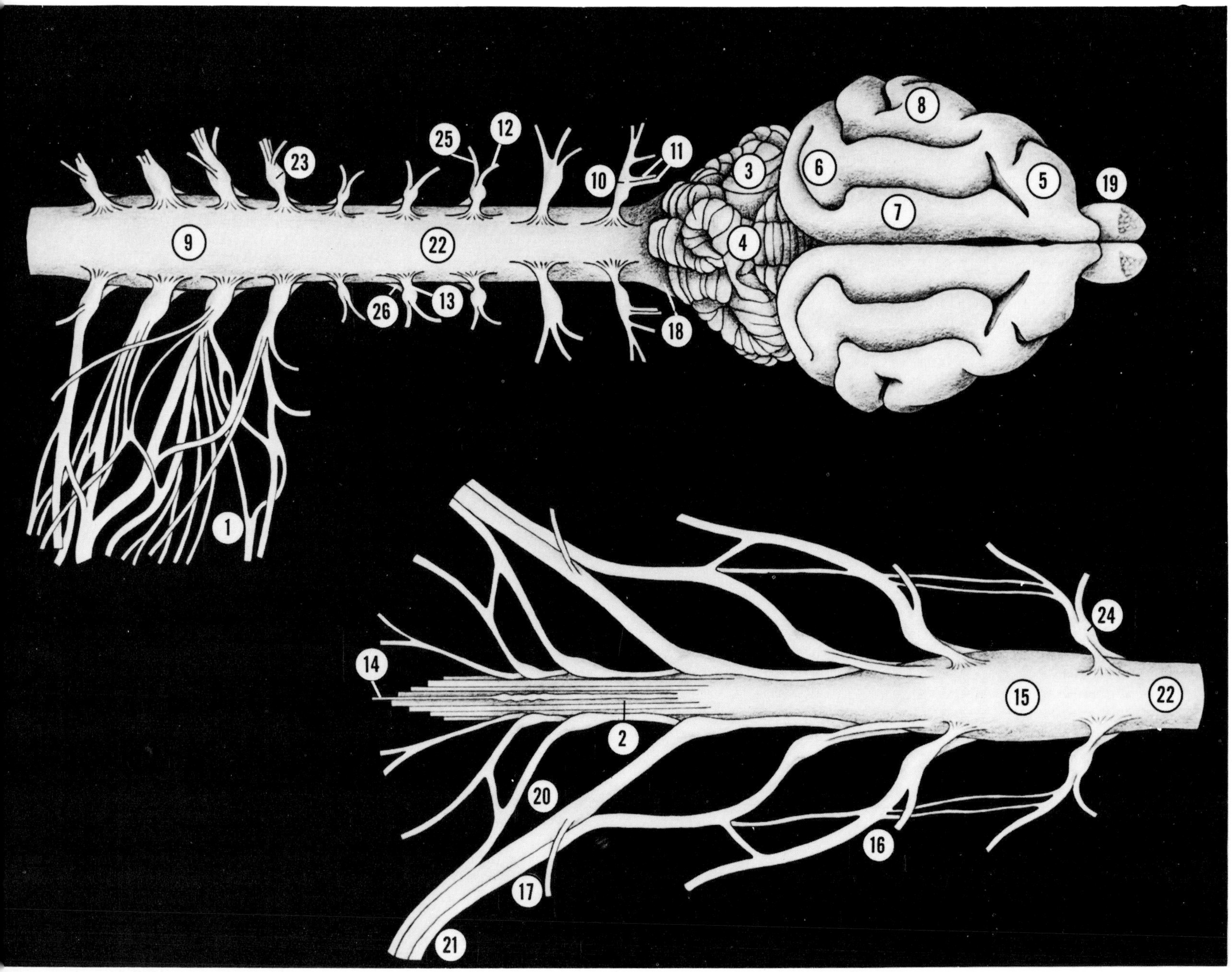

1   brachial plexus
2   cauda equina
3   **cerebellum, hemisphere**
4   cerebellum, vermis
5   **cerebral hemisphere,** frontal region
6   cerebral hemisphere, occipital region
7   cerebral hemisphere, parietal region
8   cerebral hemisphere, temporal region
9   cervical enlargement
10 cervical nerve, first
11 **communicating branches**
12 **dorsal primary division**
13 **dorsal root**
14 filum terminale
15 lumbar enlargement
16 lumbar plexus
17 lumbosacral cord
18 **medulla oblongata**
19 olfactory bulb
20 sacral plexus
21 sciatic nerve
22 **spinal cord**
23 **spinal ganglion**
24 **spinal nerve**
25 **ventral primary division**
26 **ventral root**

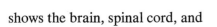

plate 54 shows the brain, spinal cord, and beginnings of spinal nerves in two portions, with dura mater removed but pia mater intact.

NERVOUS SYSTEM

composed of the **central nervous system,** which consists of **spinal cord** and **brain,** and the **peripheral nervous system,** which consists of the various **nerves,** their **afferent** and **efferent end organs,** and the **autonomic ganglia** (opposite Pl. 46).

BRAIN

opposite Plate 55.

SPINAL CORD

The mammalian spinal cord is hollow, having a very small **central canal,** which contains cerebrospinal fluid. Adjacent to the central canal is **gray substance** characterized by the presence of the **cell bodies** of the **neurons;** surrounding the gray substance is **white substance,** which never contains cell bodies but consists chiefly of nerve fibers, many of which possess **myelin sheaths,** which give the whole area a white color in fresh specimens. For details of structure the student may consult any textbook on human anatomy. The exact amount of gray and white substance varies with the various sections of the spinal cord and the parts supplied; the total size also varies, as shown by **cervical** and **lumbar enlargements,** which supply the limbs.

SPINAL NERVES

branch from the spinal cord as two roots, each consisting of several rootlets. The **dorsal root** contains **afferent fibers only** and possesses an enlargement, the **spinal ganglion,** containing all the cell bodies of the afferent fibers of that dorsal root. The **ventral root** contains **efferent fibers only,** having their cell bodies in the ventral or lateral columns of the gray substance of the spinal cord. The **spinal nerve** itself is very short, approximately the length of the intervertebral foramen through which it passes. It branches immediately into a **dorsal primary division** which supplies the dorsal areas of the back, a **ventral primary division,** which supplies most of the body wall, and one or two **communicating branches,** which supply the viscera and connect with the autonomic ganglia (opposite Pl. 46). All **branches** or **rami** of spinal nerves contain **both afferent and efferent fibers.** The spinal nerves branch from the spinal cord opposite their intervertebral foramina in young animals, but, because the spinal cord completes its growth before the vertebral column does, the posterior spinal nerves must traverse increasingly greater distances within the vertebral canal to reach their intervertebral foramina for exit. In the sacral region this is so conspicuous that the whole is termed the **cauda equina,** and the spinal cord itself dwindles to a tiny **filum terminale** near the beginning of the caudal region, in which there are usually seven or eight spinal nerves which supply the tail.

BRACHIAL PLEXUS

a network of nerves which supplies the arm and shoulder region. It usually consists of the ventral rami of the fifth to eighth cervical and first thoracic spinal nerves, which anastomose and then branch. Individual fibers never fuse when these nerves anastomose, but the fibers are regrouped and arranged in larger or smaller bundles. All plexuses show considerable variation in different specimens.

LUMBOSACRAL PLEXUS

a network of nerves which supplies the leg and pelvic region. The fourth to seventh lumbar nerves unite to form the **lumbar plexus,** and usually the three sacral nerves join with the sixth and seventh lumbar nerves to form the **sacral plexus.** A prominent part of this plexus is the large **lumbosacral cord** formed by the union of the sixth and seventh lumbar nerves. The lumbosacral cord then unites with the first sacral nerve to form the sciatic nerve (Pl. 32).

plate 55　　BRAIN, MEDIAN SECTION

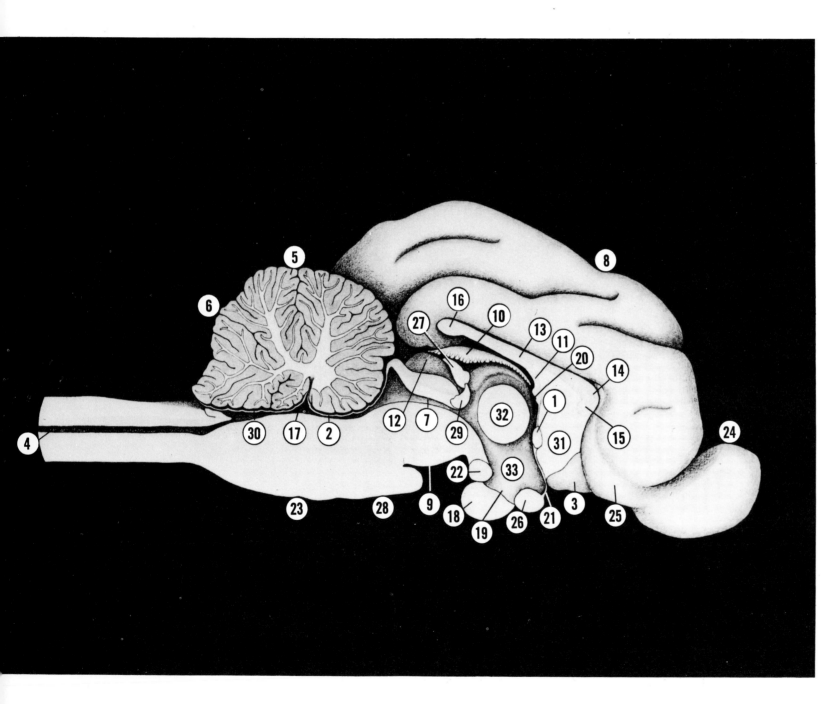

1　anterior commissure
2　anterior medullary velum
3　anterior perforated substance
4　**central canal**
5　**cerebellar cortex**
6　**cerebellum**
7　**cerebral aqueduct**
8　**cerebral hemisphere**
9　**cerebral peduncle**
10　**choroid plexus of third ventricle**
11　column of fornix
12　corpora quadrigemina, anterior colliculus
13　**corpus callosum,** body
14　corpus callosum, genu
15　corpus callosum, rostrum
16　corpus callosum, splenium
17　**fourth ventricle**
18　**hypophysis cerebri**
19　infundibulum
20　**interventricular foramen**
21　lamina terminalis
22　mammillary body
23　**medulla oblongata**
24　**olfactory bulb**
25　olfactory tract
26　optic chiasma
27　pineal body
28　**pons**
29　posterior commissure
30　posterior medullary velum
31　septum pellucidum
32　**thalamus,** intermediate mass
33　**third ventricle**

plate 55

shows the brain in median section to show the third and fourth ventricles and details of brain structure.

BRAIN

develops as a series of enlargements of the embryonic neural tube. These embryological divisions are the basis for the adult regions as follows:

A—**prosencephalon** (pross enn seff' uh lonn), or primitive forebrain
   1—**telencephalon** (tell enn seff' uh lonn), consisting of **olfactory bulbs, lamina terminalis, cerebral hemispheres** with **corpus callosum, fornix,** and two **lateral ventricles,** and the anterior end of the **third ventricle**
   2—**diencephalon** (dai enn seff' uh lonn), consisting of **thalamus, optic chiasma** and **optic tract, infundibulum** and **hypophysis cerebri, pineal body, mammillary bodies,** and **third ventricle** with its **choroid plexus**

B—**mesencephalon** (mess enn seff' uh lonn), or midbrain, consisting of **corpora quadrigemina, cerebral peduncles,** and **cerebral aqueduct**

C—**rhombencephalon** (romm benn seff' uh lonn), or hindbrain
   1—**metencephalon** (mett enn seff' uh lonn), consisting of **cerebellum** and **pons** and containing part of the **fourth ventricle**
   2—**myelencephalon** (mai eh lenn seff' uh lonn), consisting of **medulla oblongata** and most of the **fourth ventricle** with its **choroid plexus**

CEREBRUM

serr' eh brumm—variously defined; usually said to consist of all parts of the brain anterior to the metencephalon, thus including mesencephalon, diencephalon, and telencephalon.

CEREBRAL HEMISPHERE

serr' eh bral—consisting of a lateral ventricle having a greatly enlarged roof, called the **pallium** (pal' ih umm), and a basal mass, called the **corpus striatum,** which lies at the side of the thalamus. The pallium divides into white substance internally and a much-folded **cerebral cortex** of gray substance externally, which produces the apparent **gyri** (jai rai) or ridges and **sulci** or depressions. The corpus striatum includes both white and gray substance.

VENTRICLES

spaces which remain in the brain as enlargements of the embryological canal of the neural tube. The first two are not numbered but are called the **lateral ventricles,** one being found in each cerebral hemisphere and communicating with the third ventricle by the right and left **interventricular foramina.** The **third ventricle** is very narrow, located chiefly in the diencephalon but partially in the telencephalon. It contains the intermediate mass of the thalamus, which connects the two thalami by passing through the center of the ventricle from the right to the left side. The **cerebral aqueduct** passes through the mesencephalon, connecting third and fourth ventricles. The **fourth ventricle** lies in the medulla oblongata between the cerebellum and the pons, extends slightly into the cerebellum, and is continuous with the **central canal** of the spinal cord.

CHOROID PLEXUSES

koh' royd—occur in all the ventricles and are composed of the thin lining of the ventricle and the pia mater containing many small blood vessels. In the lateral ventricles the choroid plexuses invaginate from the thin medial wall; in the third ventricle the choroid plexus is located on the roof of the ventricle; while the choroid plexus of the fourth ventricle is bilateral and is located on the sides of the thin roof of the medulla oblongata just posterior to the cerebellum. **Cerebrospinal fluid,** presumably formed by choroid plexuses, circulates freely in the ventricles, central canal, and subarachnoid space (opposite Pl. 57).

plate 56   **BRAIN, VENTRAL VIEW**

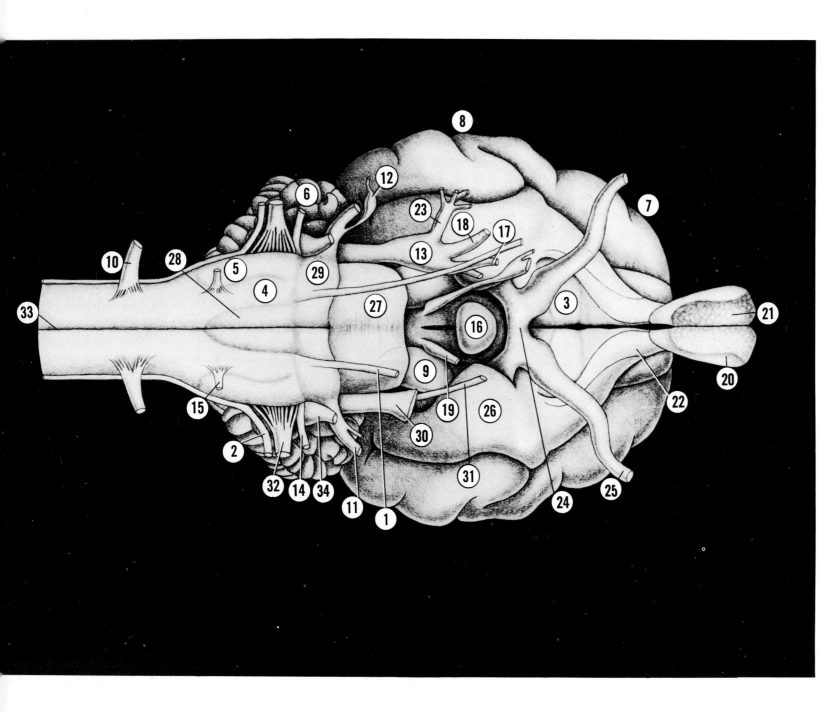

1   **abducens nerve**
2   **accessory nerve**
3   anterior perforated substance
4   area elliptica
5   area ovalis
6   cerebellum, hemisphere
7   cerebral hemisphere, frontal region
8   cerebral hemisphere, temporal region
9   **cerebral peduncle**
10   cervical nerve, first
11   **facial nerve**
12   ganglion, geniculate
13   ganglion, trigeminal
14   **glossopharyngeal nerve**
15   **hypoglossal nerve**
16   **hypophysis cerebri**
17   mandibular nerve
18   maxillary nerve
19   **oculomotor nerve**
20   olfactory bulb
21   **olfactory nerves,** cut
22   olfactory tract
23   ophthalmic nerve
24   **optic chiasma**
25   **optic nerve**
26   piriform area
27   **pons**
28   pyramid
29   trapezium
30   **trigeminal nerve**
31   **trochlear nerve**
32   **vagus nerve**
33   ventral median fissure
34   **vestibulocochlear nerve**

plate 56

shows the brain and cranial nerves in ventral view.

HYPOPHYSIS CEREBRI

hai poff' ih siss—or pituitary gland. An endocrine gland which forms many important hormones and is derived embryologically from the brain and the roof of the mouth.

CEREBRAL PEDUNCLES

peh dunng' kehls—large tracts connecting the cerebral hemispheres with the rest of the central nervous system and comprising the floor of the mesencephalon.

CRANIAL NERVES

The components of nerves: The fibers within a nerve can be classified according to the function they serve. Four types of components are present in spinal nerves, designated GENERAL to differentiate them from special components in cranial nerves. Two are afferent, **general somatic afferent** (sensory from somatic structures, such as body wall, muscles, tendons), and **general visceral afferent,** (sensory from glands, smooth and cardiac muscle). Two are efferent, **general somatic efferent** (motor to striated muscle), and **general visceral efferent** (motor to glands, smooth and cardiac muscle).

Cranial nerves may also have these general components and in addition three SPECIAL categories are identified as follows: **special somatic afferent** (for fibers carrying special senses of sight, hearing and equilibrium); **special visceral afferent** (for special sense of taste, associated with visceral functions); **special visceral efferent** (for nerve fibers motor to muscles of branchiomeric origin, which is associated with visceral activities). The cranial nerves with their functional components are as follows.

I—Olfactory, special visceral afferent from the nasal mucosa to the olfactory bulb. The fibers course through the cribriform plate of the ethmoid bone.

II—Optic, special somatic afferent from the retina to the optic chiasma to the diencephalon. Only the fibers from the medial regions of the retina cross to the opposite side of the brain in the optic chiasma.

III—Oculomotor, general somatic efferent from mesencephalon to the muscles of the eyeball and upper eyelid. General visceral efferent from mesencephalon to the involuntary muscles of the eye.

IV—Trochlear, general somatic efferent from region of anterior medullary velum in mesencephalon to superior oblique muscle of eyeball.

V—Trigeminal, general somatic afferent from skin, mucous membrane and teeth to the pons. Special visceral efferent from pons to muscles of mastication. The Trigeminal Nerve is composed of three large branches: ophthalmic (off thal' mick) or profundus, maxillary and mandibular, which course to the large Trigeminal Ganglion (semilunar). A small efferent root follows the mandibular branch.

VI—Abducens, general somatic efferent from medulla oblongata to lateral rectus muscles of eyeball.

VII—Facial, general somatic afferent from skin of ear to medulla oblongata; general visceral afferent from tongue and floor of mouth to trapezium in medulla; special visceral afferent from tongue to medulla; general visceral efferent from medulla to the glands of mouth, nose and pharynx; special visceral efferent from medulla to muscles of the face.

VIII—Vestibulocochlear (Acoustic), special somatic afferent from ear to medulla oblongata.

IX—Glossopharyngeal, general somatic afferent from skin of ear to medulla oblongata; general visceral afferent from pharynx and tongue to medulla; special visceral efferent from medulla to stylopharyngeus muscle in pharynx.

X—Vagus, general somatic afferent from skin of ear to medulla oblongata; general visceral afferent from pharynx, larynx, and thoracic and abdominal viscera; special visceral afferent from the region of the epiglottic taste buds to medulla; general visceral efferent from medulla to involuntary muscles of viscera; special visceral efferent from medulla to certain muscles of the pharynx and larynx.

XI—Accessory, special visceral efferent from medulla oblongata to muscles moving the shoulder, head and some muscles of the pharynx. This nerve is composed of a spinal and a cranial portion. The spinal portion consists of many small rootlets from the lateral surface of the medulla and spinal cord posteriorly as far as the seventh cervical nerve. These rootlets unite to form the main trunk of the nerve which passes anteriorly through the foramen magnum into the cranial cavity where rootlets from the cranial portion in the medulla unite with it. The entire nerve emerges from the skull through the jugular foramen and divides, one part supplying the cleidomastoid, sternomastoid, levator scapulae ventralis and trapezius muscles; the other part distributes with the vagus nerve.

XII—Hypoglossal, general somatic efferent from medulla oblongata at lateral edge of area elliptica to muscles of tongue.

plate 57

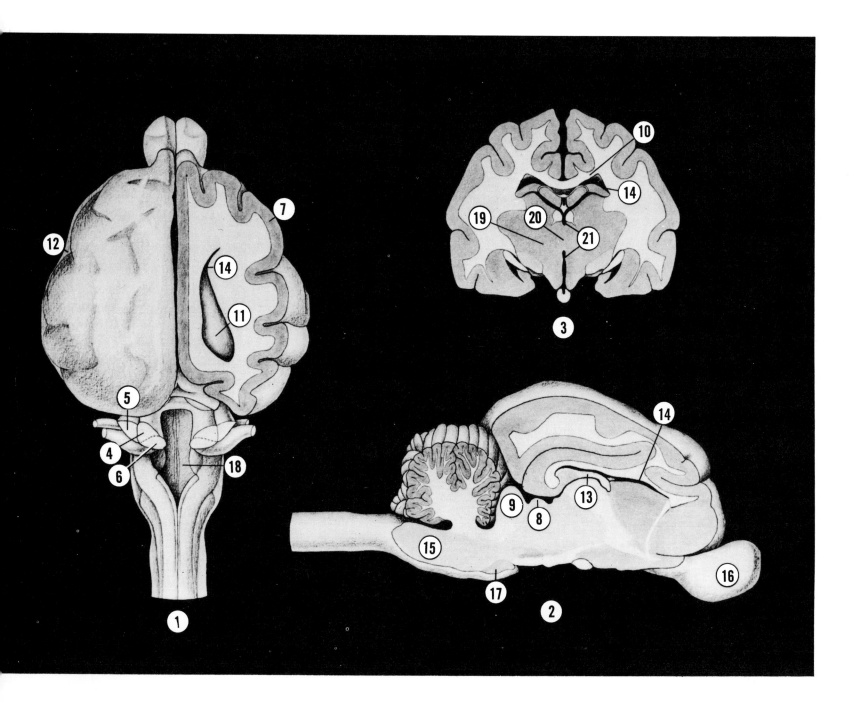

1 **brain with cerebellum removed, dorsal view**
2 **brain with cerebral hemisphere cut sagittally, lateral view**
3 **brain, transverse section through third ventricle**
4 **cerebellar peduncle, anterior**
5 **cerebellar peduncle, middle**
6 **cerebellar peduncle, posterior**
7 **cerebral cortex**
8 corpora quadrigemina, anterior colliculus
9 corpora quadrigemina, posterior colliculus
10 corpus callosum
11 corpus striatum
12 **dura mater**
13 fornix
14 **lateral ventricle**
15 **medulla oblongata**
16 olfactory bulb
17 pons
18 rhomboid fossa of fourth ventricle
19 thalamus
20 thalamus, intermediate mass
21 **third ventricle**

plate 57

shows the brain cut to expose internal structures. In Figure 1 the cerebellum has been removed to expose the cerebellar peduncles, and a horizontal cut has been made through the right cerebral hemisphere to show its lateral ventricle, while the dura mater has been left intact on the left cerebral hemisphere. Figure 2 shows a lateral view of the brain, with a sagittal cut through the right cerebral hemisphere, exposing the right lateral ventricle. In Figure 3 a transverse cut has been made through the diencephalon to show the very narrow third ventricle.

CORPUS CALLOSUM

kah loh′ summ—a wide band of fibers which connects right and left cerebral hemispheres. It is dorsal to the thin roof or choroid plexus of the third ventricle.

THALAMUS

thal′ uh muss—consists mostly of gray substance. There are two thalami, one on each side of the third ventricle; they are connected by the intermediate mass which passes through the third ventricle.

CORPUS STRIATUM

strai ay′ tumm—is found on the floor of each lateral ventricle and consists mostly of gray substance. The corpora striata lie at the sides of the thalami.

CORPORA QUADRIGEMINA

kor′ poh ruh kwodd rih jemm′ ih nuh—consist of two **anterior colliculi** and two **posterior colliculi.** The anterior colliculi are homologous to the optic lobes of more primitive vertebrates, while the posterior colliculi are considered to be new elevations concerned mainly with auditory sensations.

MENINGES

meh ninn′ jeez—of the brain and spinal cord are the **dura mater** (diu′ ruh may′ terr), **arachnoid coat,** and **pia mater** (pai′ uh). The **dura mater** is tough, fibrous, heavy connective tissue, lying adjacent to the skull and vertebral canal, while the **pia mater** is very thin, closely follows the outline of the spinal cord and subdivisions of the brain, including their minute sulci, and conveys small blood vessels to the nerve tissue. The **arachnoid coat** is too thin to be seen in dissection of the cat brain but lies close to the dura mater, leaving a **subarachnoid space** between the arachnoid coat and the pia mater. This space is filled with **cerebrospinal fluid,** which is considered to be formed chiefly by the choroid plexuses of the four ventricles of the brain (opposite Pl. 55). In man this fluid is known to pass through three small foramina in the roof of the fourth ventricle to the subarachnoid space; presumably, a similar mechanism exists in the cat. The cerebrospinal fluid is very watery, more so than lymph, and circulates freely from the ventricles and central canal inside the central nervous system to the subarachnoid space, which surrounds the brain and spinal cord. The cerebrospinal fluid is absorbed by the blood stream through the arachnoid villi into large venous sinuses between the skull and the dura mater, and there is probably a fairly rapid rate of continuous production and loss of this fluid.

GLOSSARY

In the glossary are presented pronunciations, synonymous terms, derivations, and definitions in the order given. The letter symbols following the synonymous terms are those used in the introduction; they are: NA for Nomina Anatomica (3rd ed., Wiesbaden, 1965), BNA for Basle Nomina Anatomica, NK for a modification of the BNA, BR for the British Revision, INA for the revision begun by the International Congress of Anatomists, OT for old terminology used before the BNA. The pronunciation system is a visual one so that the student will be able to understand the pronunciation without knowing a set of diacritical marks. In general, the system uses combinations of letters which have familiar sounds. The accompanying table lists the symbols most often used for the common vowel sounds.

VOWEL	SYMBOL*	PRONOUNCED AS IN
ā	ay	ale
ē	ee	eve
ī	ai	ice
ō	oh	old
ū	iu	cube
ă	a followed by a doubled consonant (except with *l* and *r*)	add
ĕ	eh if final letter in syllable, otherwise *e* followed by a doubled consonant	end
ĭ	ih if final letter in syllable, otherwise *i* followed by a doubled consonant	ill
ŏ	ah if final letter in syllable, otherwise *o* followed by a doubled consonant	odd
ŭ	uh if final letter in syllable, otherwise *u* followed by a doubled consonant	up
ä	ah (exception *arr*)	arm

* It is impossible in a system without diacritical marks to represent exactly all the shades of vowel sounds; therefore, exceptions to the system as here given were occasionally necessary. For example, the sound of *ī* followed by *n* has been given as *-ine* instead of *-ain* to avoid the connotation in such words as *attain*, the sound of *ô* before *r* has been simply represented as *or* and *ck* has been used instead of the doubled consonant, *kk*.

abdominal ostium, uterine tube—NA, BNA, pelvic opening, BR, abdominal opening, ostium tubae, ostium tubae abdominale.

abducens nerve abb diu′ senns—NA, BNA. L. *abducere*, to lead away. Supplies lateral rectus muscle, which pulls eyeball laterally. Cranial Nerve VI.

abduct—L. *abducere*, from *ab*, away, + *ducere*, to lead. To draw away from a median axis.

abductor muscle—a muscle which pulls away from a median axis.

accessory nerve—NA, BNA, spinal accessory nerve, OT. Cranial Nerve XI.

accessory process—NA, anapophysis. L. *ana* back, + *apophysis*, offshoot.

acetabular bone ass eh tabb′ iu lerr—cotyloid bone, OT.

acetabulum ass eh tabb′ iu lumm—cotyloid cavity, OT. L. little vinegar cup.

acoustic nerve uh koos′ tick—see vestibulocochlear nerve.

acromiodeltoideus muscle—acromiodeltoid.

acromion uh kroh′ mih ɵn—NA, BNA, acromion process, OT. G. *akros*, tip or point, + *omos*, shoulder.

acromiotrapezius muscle—trapezius superior.

adduct—L. *adducere*, from *ad*, to, + *ducere*, to lead. To draw toward a median axis.

adductor muscle—a muscle which pulls toward a median axis.

adenoids add′ eh noyds—G. *adenoides*, from *aden*, gland, + *eidos*, resemblance. An enlarged pharyngeal tonsil; usually used only in the plural.

adrenal gland—see **suprarenal gland.**

afferent—L. *affere*, from *ad*, to, + *ferre*, to carry. Afferent nerve fibers take nerve impulses toward the central nervous system.

ali—L. *ala*, wing, winglike; a combining form.

allantochorion ah lann′ toh koh′ rih ɵn—fused chorion and allantois.

allantois ah lann′ toh iss′—a fetal membrane.

alveolus al vee′ oh luss; pl. **alveoli** al vee′ oh lai—L. a small hollow or cavity.

amnion amm′ nih on—the innermost fetal membrane.

anal ay′ nal—L. *anus*, a ring.

anapophysis—see **accessory process.**

anastomosis uh nass toh moh′ sis—G. *ana*, up, + *stoma*, mouth, an opening-up; *anastomoun*, to furnish with a mouth. A communication between blood vessels of the same type.

anconeus muscle ang koh′ nee′ uss; ang koh′ nee uss—NA, BNA, anconeus quartus, OT. L. *ancon*, elbow.

antebrachium ann teh bray′ kih umm; ann teh brack′ ih umm—L. *ante*, before, + *brachium*, arm from shoulder to elbow. The forearm between elbow and wrist; also sometimes spelled antibrachium, though contrary to its derivation.

anterior articular process—superior articular process, NA, BNA, cranial articular process, NK, prezygapophysis.

anterior articular surface—cranial articular surface, INA, superior articular facet or surface, BNA, BR.

anterior cervical ganglion—superior cervical ganglion, NA, BNA.

anterior commissure komm′ ih shur; komm′ ih sur—NA, commissura anterior cerebri, BNA. A bundle of white fibers crossing between the two thalami.

anterior epigastric artery—superior epigastric, NA, BNA. Posterior continuation of internal thoracic artery lateral to rectus abdominis muscle, and anastomosing with the posterior epigastric artery.

anterior ganglion of vagus nerve—jugular ganglion, BNA, superior ganglion, NA, BR. A small enlargement on the vagus nerve in the jugular foramen.

anterior gluteal artery—superior gluteal, NA, BNA.

anterior gluteal vein—superior gluteal, NA, BNA. Parallels anterior gluteal artery.

anterior mesenteric artery—superior mesenteric, NA, BNA.

anterior mesenteric ganglion—superior mesenteric, NA, BNA.

anterior mesenteric vein—superior mesenteric, NA, BNA.

anterior nasal aperture—NA, BR, piriform aperture, BNA. Anterior nasal opening in the skull. Naris or anterior naris are also used, but they more correctly refer to the external opening of the entire nose, including the cartilages.

anterior thoracic artery—NA, arteria thoracalis suprema, BNA, superior thoracic.

anterior vena cava—superior vena cava, NA, BNA, cranial vena cava, NK, descending vena cava, precava, precaval vein.

aorta ay or′ tuh—G. perhaps from *aeirein*, to lift up or be hung; "the artery from which the heart hangs."

aortic valve—NA, BR, NK, valvuae semilunares aortae, BNA, semilunar valve of aorta.

aperture app′ err tiur—L. *aperire*, to uncover, open; an opening.

aponeurosis app oh niu roh′ sis; pl. **aponeuroses** app oh niu roh′ seez—G. *apo*, from, + *neuron*, which before Aristotle meant anything of a fibrous nature. A flat, sheetlike fibrous attachment of a muscle; a flat tendon.

arachnoid uh rack′ noyd—G. *arachnoides*, like a cobweb.

area elliptica—not found in man; perhaps homologous to the olive, NA, oliva, BNA, or olivary eminence.

area ovalis—not found in man.

artery—G. *aer,* air, + *terein,* to keep; L. *arteria.* Ancients thought arteries were windpipes, because they were empty in dead animals.

articular process—NA, BNA, zygapophysis.

articular surface or facet—NA, BNA, INA, BR.

aryepiglottic fold—NA, BNA, ary-epiglottic, arytenoepiglottic, aryepiglottidean. Between arytenoid cartilages and epiglottis.

atavistic att uh viss' tick—pertaining to reversion to a more primitive type.

atlas—from Greek mythology, Atlas supported the heavens; name introduced by Vesalius; prior to that, it had been known as the epistropheus (Jayne).

atrioventricular groove—NA, BR, coronary sulcus, BNA, auriculoventricular groove, OT. Marks the line of division between atria and ventricles of the heart.

atrioventricular valve—NA; left, bicuspid; right, tricuspid.

atrium ay' trih umm—NA, BNA, auricle, OT. L. antechamber.

auditory capsule—layer of connective tissue surrounding the embryonic otocyst, which becomes cartilaginous, and is later replaced by bone in all higher vertebrates.

auditory ossicles—NA, BNA, bones of the middle ear: the incus, malleus and stapes.

auditory tube—NA, pharyngotympanic tube, BR, Eustachian tube, OT.

auricle—NA, BNA, auricular appendage, OT. Also old terminology for atrium, BNA. L. little ear.

auricular surface oh rick' iu lerr—L. *auricula,* dim of *auris,* ear. Facet on the ilium or sacrum for articulation; so named because in man it is supposed to be shaped like an ear.

automatic nervous system—sympathetic plus parasympathetic systems, NA, IANC.

axilla ack sill' uh—L. *axilla,* the armpit.

axillary ack' sih lerr ih, ack sill' uh rih.

axis—NA, BR, epistropheus, BNA. The name epistropheus epp ih stroh' feh uss, G. *epi,* upon, + *strephein,* to turn, was given to axis by Heister (1683–1758) some time after it had been abandoned as the name of the atlas (Jayne).

axon ack' sonn—axone, neurite, axis cylinder if sheathed. G. *axon,* axis. A long, thin, relatively unbranched nerve process; also used for a process which conducts impulses away from the cell body.

azygos vein azz' ih goss—azygous. G. *azygos,* from *a,* not, + *zygon,* yoke; unpaired.

basi—G. *basis,* base; a combining form.

basihyal bone—also called the body of the hyoid bone. This bone is a cross bar which connects the two sides of the hyoid apparatus of the cat, articulating with ceratohyal and thyrohyal bones.

biceps brachii muscle bai' sepps bray' kih ai; brack' ih ai—NA, BNA, biceps humeri, OT, biceps flexor OT, biceps.

biceps femoris muscle bai' sepps femm' oh riss—NA, BNA, biceps flexor cruris, OT.

bicipital groove—see **intertubercular groove.**

bicuspid valve—see **atrioventricular valve,** left.

body cavity—usually defined as that cavity bounded by the body wall and containing the viscera, whereas the celom lies between viscera and body wall.

brachialis muscle bray kih ay' liss; brack ih ay' liss—NA, BNA, brachialis anticus, OT.

brachiocephalic artery—NA, artery anonyma, BNA, innominate artery, OT. L. *innominatus,* unnamed. Galen described, but did not name it; Vesalius called it the "unnamed" artery.

brachioradialis muscle bray' kih oh ray dih ay' liss; brack' ih oh ray dih ay' liss—NA, BNA, supinator longus, OT.

brachium bray' kih umm; brack' ih umm—upper segment of arm from shoulder to elbow.

brachium pontis—see **cerebellar peduncle,** middle.

bronchial brong' kih al.

bulbourethral gland buhl boh iu ree' thral—NA, BNA, Cowper's gland, OT.

bulla bull' uh; pl. **bullae** bull' ee—L. *bulla,* a bubble.

calcaneus kal kay' neh uss—NA, BNA, calcaneum, BR, os calcis, calx, os tarsi fibulare, NK. L. heel. Bone of the heel.

canal (or foramen) of auditory tube—NA, osseous portion of auditory tube, BNA, canal of the pharyngotympanic tube, BR.

capitate bone kapp' ih tayt—NA, os capitatum, BNA, os magnum, OT. L. *capitatus,* from *caput,* head.

capitulum kuh pitt' iu lumm—L. *caput,* head, + dim. *-ulum,* small head.

carotid kuh rott' idd—G. *karoun,* to put to sleep, or *karotides,* heavy sleep. Early Greeks found pressure on these arteries caused goats to lose consciousness.

carpal bones—carpus, G. *karpos,* wrist.

carpale kahr pay' lee; pl. **carpalia** kahr pay' lih uh—one of the bones in the distal row of carpal bones.

cauda equina kah' dah eh kwai nuh—composed of the tapering end of the spinal cord and the elongated spinal nerves, because the adult spinal cord does not extend below the first lumbar vertebra in man. They form a bundle likened to a horse's tail.

caudal—L. *cauda,* tail, of, or pertaining to the tail.

caudal articular process—see **posterior articular process.**

caudal articular surface—see **posterior articular surface.**

caudofemoralis muscle kah doh femm oh ray' liss.

cecum see' kumm; pl. **ceca** see' kuh— caecum, the ileocolic cecum. L. *caecus,* blind; a blind pouch or sac.

celiac see' lih ack— coeliac, L. *coeliacus,* from G. *koiliakos,* hollow, or G. *koila,* belly.

celiac ganglion see' lih ack—NA, BNA, semilunar ganglion, solar ganglion, OT.

celiac plexus—NA, BNA, coeliac plexus, solar plexus, epigastric plexus, OT.

cell body of a neuron—cell body, cyton, perikaryon. That portion of a cell which encloses the nucleus, as distinguished from its processes.

celom see' lomm—coelom, coelome. G. *koiloma,* a hollow. The body cavity, which is lined by an epithelium derived from mesoderm.

cephalo- seff' uh loh—G. *kephale,* head; a combining form.

cerato- serr' uh toh—G. *keras,* horn; a combining form.

ceratohyal bone serr uh toh hai' al—hypohyal, lesser horn. The lesser horn of the hyoid bone of man is said to be homologous to the ceratohyal of lower forms.

cerebellar peduncle, anterior serr eh bell' err peh dunng' kehl—NA, brachium conjunctivum, BNA, superior cerebellar peduncle, BR, crus cerebello-cerebrale, NK. Fibers from cerebellum to mesencephalon.

cerebellar peduncle, middle—NA, BR, brachium pontis, BNA, crus ponto-cerebellare, NK. L. *brachium,* arm, + *pons,* bridge. Fibers from pons to cerebellum.

cerebellar peduncle, posterior—NA, inferior cerebellar peduncle, BR, corpus restiforme, BNA, BR, crus medullo-cerebellare, NK. L. *restis,* rope + *forma,* like; a ropelike body.

cerebellum serr eh bell' umm—L. dim. of *cerebrum;* little brain.

cerebral aqueduct serr' eh bral—NA, BNA, aqueduct of midbrain, BR, NK, aqueduct of Sylvius, OT.

cerebrum serr' eh brumm.

cervical—L. *cervix,* neck; therefore, of or pertaining to the neck.

chiasmatic groove—NA, sulcus chiasmatis, BNA; optic groove, OT; for the optic chiasma.

chevron bone—shaped like a chevron, and encloses caudal artery and vein. Variously considered to be homologous to hemal arches, hypocentra, basiventrals, or intercentra.

choana koh' uh nuh; pl. **choanae** koh' uh nee—NA, BNA, posterior aperture of the nose, BR, posterior naris, internal naris, OT. Openings of nasal cavities into nasopharynx.

choledoch duct—see common bile duct.

chondrocranium konn droh kray' nih umm—the cartilaginous brain case, which occurs in the adult stage of lower forms such as the dogfish, but occurs only in early developmental stages of most vertebrates.

chorda tendinea kor' duh tenn dinn' eh uh; pl. **chordae tendineae** kor' dee tenn dinn' eh ee.

choroid plexus koh' royd.

clavicle klavv' ih kehl—L. *clavicula,* a little key, from *clavis,* key.

clavobrachialis muscle klay voh bray kih ay' liss; klay voh brach ih ay' liss—clavodeltoid.

clitoris klai' toh riss; klitt' oh riss.

collateral ganglia—prevertebral ganglia.

colliculus, anterior kah lick' iu luss—superior colliculus, NA, BNA, colliculus cranialis, NK, colliculus rostralis, INA, superior quadrigemeinal body, BR. L. a little hill.

colliculus, posterior—inferior colliculus, NA, BNA, colliculus caudalis, NK, INA, inferior quadrigeminal body, BR.

common bile duct—NA, choledoch duct koll′ eh dock, choledochal duct, ductus choledochus, BNA, ductus communis choledochus. G. *choledochos,* from *chole,* bile, + *dochos,* containing.

common iliac vein—formed by union of external iliac and internal iliac veins.

common peroneal nerve perr oh nee′ al—NA, nervus peronaeus communis, BNA, nervus fibularis communis, INA, external popliteal nerve.

communicating branch of spinal nerve—NA, communicating ramus, visceral branch or rami communicantes. May be either white, composed of myelinated preganglionic fibers, or gray, composed of unmyelinated postganglionic fibers.

concha kong′ kuh; pl. **conchae** kong′ kee—NA, BNA, nasal concha, turbinated bone, turbinal, OT.

condyle konn′ dill—L. *condylus,* knuckle, joint; an articular prominence on a bone.

condyloid canal—posterior condyloid foramen. For the passage of a vein.

coracobrachialis muscle kor′ uh koh bray kih ay′ liss; kor′ uh koh brack ih ay′ liss.

coracoid kor′ uh koyd—G. *korax,* raven, + *eidos,* form; like a raven's beak. A cartilage or bone of the pectoral girdle, reduced to a process in mammals above the monotremes.

coronal suture koh roh′ nal; kor′ oh nal—L. *corona,* a crown.

coronoid kor′ oh noyd—G. *korone,* crow, + *eidos,* form; like a crow's beak.

corpora quadrigemina kor′ poh ruh kwodd rih jemm′ ih nuh—L. *corpora,* bodies, + *quadri,* four + *geminus,* twin; four bodies.

corpus callosum—L. *callosus,* hard. The great transverse commissure between the cerebral hemispheres lying at the bottom of the longitudinal fissure.

corpus luteum kor′ puss liu teh umm; pl. **corpora lutea** kor′ poh ruh liu teh uh—L. yellow body.

corpus spongiosum penis—NA, BR, corpus cavernosum urethrae, BNA, corpus spongiosum, OT.

corpus striatum kor′ pus strai ay′ tumm; pl. **corpora striata** kor′ poh ruh strai ay′ tuh—NA. Either of a pair of large masses of the brain located beneath and lateral to the anterior horns of the lateral ventricles. Each consists of a caudate and lentiform nucleus, the striated appearance being caused by bands of gray substance passing through the internal capsule which separates these two nuclei.

cortex—L. bark; outer region of an organ.

costal kohs′ tal—L. *costa;* of, or pertaining to the ribs.

costal cartilage—sternal rib. Connects rib to sternum directly or indirectly, and is the unossified portion of the rib of the fetus.

costal facet—NA, BR, costal pit, BNA.

craniad kray′ nih add—G. *kranion,* head; directed toward the head.

cranial kray′ nih al—G. *kranion,* head; of or pertaining to the skull.

cranial articular process—see **anterior articular process.**

cranial articular surface—see **anterior articular surface.**

craniosacral division of the autonomic nervous system kray nih oh say′ kral—see **parasympathetic nervous system.**

cribriform plate kribb′ rih form—L. *cribrum,* sieve, + *form,* like; sievelike. Allows for passage of the many parts of the olfactory nerve.

crus of penis kruss; pl. **crura** kroo′ ruh—L. fleshy part of the leg.

cuneiform bones of foot kiu nee′ ih form; kiu′ neh ih form—medial, intermediate, lateral, NA, first, second, third, BNA; internal, middle, external, OT. L. *cuneus,* a wedge, + *forma,* form.

cystic duct—L. *cystis,* from G. *kystis,* bladder. Duct leading to and from the gall bladder.

deep femoral vein—NA, vena profunda femoralis BNA. Parallels deep femoral artery.

dendrite—dendron, dendritic process. G. *dendron,* tree. A short branching process of a nerve cell; also used for a process which conducts impulses to the cell body.

dens dennz—NA, BNA, odontoid process BR. L. tooth.

dentition, deciduous deh sidd′ iu uss—NA, BNA, milk, dentition, temporary dentition. L. *decidere,* to fall off.

diaphragm dai′ uh framm—G. *diaphragm,* a wall or partition, from *dia,* across, + *phragma,* a wall.

diencephalon dai enn seff′ uh lonn—between brain, thalamencephalon, interbrain.

digitigrade dihj′ ih tih grayd—L. *digitus,* finger or toe, + *gradi,* to walk; walking upon the digits.

dorsal—L. *dorsualis,* from *dorsum,* back; of, or pertaining to the back.

dorsal primary division of a spinal nerve—NA, dorsal ramus, NK, posterior ramus, BNA, BR. It supplies the dorsal portion of the body wall.

dorsal nasal concha—superior nasal concha, NA, BNA, superior turbinal, OT, nasoturbinal, ethmoturbinal, if homologous to that of man.

dorsal root of a spinal nerve—NA, NK, posterior root, BNA, BR. Contains only afferent fibers.

dorsum sellae dor′ summ sell′ ee—L. back of a seat. The back of the sella turcica.

duct of the cochlea kock′ leh uh—NA, BR, BNA, scala media, membrane cochlea, OT.

ductus choledochus kah ledd′ oh kuss—see **common bile duct.**

ductus deferens duck′ tuss deff′ err ennz—NA, BNA, deferent duct, vas deferens. BR, OT. L. *deferens,* carrying down.

duodenal papilla diu oh dee′ nal puh pill′ uh—NA, BNA, ampulla of Vater, bile papilla. Santorini's papilla, OT.

duodenum diu oh dee′ numm—L. *duodeni,* twelve. So named because of its length in man of fingerbreadths.

dura mater diu′ ruh may′ terr—L. hard or strong mother. "The membrane was called mater after the Arabic usage of words for father and mother, because it was thought to give rise to every membrane in the body" (Webster).

efferent eff′ err ennt—L. *effere,* to bear out, from *ex,* out, from, + *ferre,* to carry. Efferent nerve fibers take nerve impulses from the central nervous system to a muscle or gland; efferent neurons possess efferent fibers.

efferent ductules—NA, ductuli efferentes testis, BNA, vasa efferentia.

end organ—Either afferent or efferent. Specialized ending of a nerve fiber, usually with accessory structures.

epi—G. *epi,* on, upon; a combining form.

epididymis epp ih didd′ ih miss—G. *epididymis,* from *epi,* upon, + *didymos,* testis.

epiglottis epp ih glott′ iss—G. *epi,* upon, + *glotta,* tongue.

epihyal bone—epp ih hai′ al—a bone of the anterior horn of the hyoid bone of the cat. It is thought to be represented in man by the stylohyoid ligament.

epiphysis eh piff′ ih siss; pl. **epiphyses** eh piff′ ih seez—G. *epi,* upon, + *physis,* growth.

epiploic foramen epp ih ploh′ ick—NA, BNA, opening into lesser peritoneal sac, BR, foramen of Winslow, OT. G. *epiploon,* the omentum.

epistropheus—see **axis**

epitrochlearis muscle epp ih trock leh ay′ riss—extensor antebrachii, extensor antebrachii longus.

esophageal artery ee soh faj′ eh al; eh soff uh jee′ al.

esophagus eh soff′ uh guss—G. *oisophagus,* from *oiso,* I shall carry, + *phagein,* to eat.

ethmoid bone—G. ethmos, a sieve, + *eidos,* form; like a sieve.

ethmoturbinal—see **middle nasal concha.**

extensor carpi radialis brevis muscle karr′ pai ray dih ay′ liss bree′ viss—NA, brevior, BNA, radialis externus brevis, OT.

extensor carpi radialis longus muscle long′ guss—NA longior, BNA radialis externus longus, OT.

extensor digiti minimi muscle—NA, extensor digiti quinti proprius, BNA.

extensor digitorum muscle dihj ih toh′ rumm—NA extensor digitorum communis, BNA.

extensor digitorum lateralis muscle—BNA. Said to correspond in position to the extensor digiti minimus of man.

extensor digitorum longus muscle—BNA.

extensor indicis muscle inn′ dih sis—NA, extensor indicis proprius, BNA, indicator muscle, OT. Used when we straighten the index finger in pointing at an object.

external abdominal oblique muscle obb leek′; obb laik′—NA, BNA, obliquus abdominis externus, INA.

external acoustic meatus meh ay′ tuss—NA, BNA, external auditory meatus, BR.

external iliac vein—parallels external iliac artery.

external uterine orifice—NA, BNA, os uteri externum, BR, external os uteri, orificium externum isthmi, NK.

facet fass′ ett—French, facette, a little face.

falciform ligament fal′ sih form—NA, ligamentum falciforme hepatis, BNA, suspensory ligament, broad ligament of the liver, OT. L. *falx, falcis,* sickle, + *form,* sickle-shaped.

fascia fassh′ ih uh; pl. **fasciae** fassh′ ih ee—L. a band. A thin sheet of tough, fibrous connective tissue, often found encasing organs or muscle groups.

fascia lata fassh ih uh lay tuh—NA, BNA, broad fascia.

fasciculus fah sick′ iu luss—L. dim. of *fascis*, bundle. A slender bundle of fibers, as of muscle fibers or nerve fibers.

femoral vein femm′ oh ral—parallels femoral artery.

femur, greater trochanter troh kann′ terr—NA, BNA. *G. trochanter*, from *trachein*, to run; a runner.

femur, intercondylar fossa—NA, intercondyloid fossa, BNA, intercondylic, intercondylous, intercondylar notch, BR.

fetus fee′ tuss; pl. **fetuses**—foetus. L. offspring. Young after developed sufficiently to make the species distinguishable. Termed embryo before this.

fibula fibb′ iu luh—first term for this bone was *perone*, a pin, used by Greeks for bone of ox, etc. Hippocrates used it for man. Vesalius used *fibula* as a translation of *perone*, because Romans called pins *fibulae* (Jayne). L. fastener. Calf bone.

filiform papillae fill′ ih form; fai′ lai form—L. *filum*, thread; threadlike.

filum terminale fai′ lumm terr mih nay′ lee—L. terminal thread. The slender posterior end of the spinal cord.

flex—L. to bend.

flexor carpi radialis muscle fleck′ sorr karr′ pai ray dih ay′ liss—NA, BNA, radialis internus, OT.

flexor carpi ulnaris muscle ull nay′ riss—NA, BNA, ulnaris internus, OT.

flexor digitorum longus muscle fleck′ sorr dihj ih toh′ rumm long′ guss—NA, BNA, flexor longus digitorum, OT.

flexor digitorum profundus muscle proh funn′ duss—NA, BNA, flexor profundus digitorum, perforans, OT.

flexor hallucis longus muscle hah liu′ sis—NA, BNA, flexor longus hallucis, OT.

foramen foh ray′ menn; pl. **foramina** foh ramm′ ih nuh—L. *forare*, to bore; a small opening.

foramen magnum magg′ numm—occipital foramen, OT.

foramen ovale oh vay′ lee—for the mandibular division of the trigeminal nerve.

foramen rotundum roh tunn′ dumm—for the maxillary division of the trigeminal nerve.

fornix for′ nicks; pl. **fornices** for′ nih seez—L. arch, vault. Arched, paired fiber tracts joined medially under the corpus callosum and lying above the choroid plexus of the third ventricle. They connect hippocampus and mammillary body on each side.

fossa fahs′ uh; pl. **fossae** fahs′ ee—L. a ditch. A pit, cavity, or depression.

fovea capitis femoris foh veh′ ih kapp′ ih tiss femm′ oh riss—NA, BNA, pit for ligament of head of femur, BR.

frontal bone, zygomatic process—NA, BNA, postorbital process.

frontal suture—the suture between the two frontal bones and continuous with the sagittal suture; not normally present in man.

fungiform papillae funn′ jih form—resembling a mushroom.

gall bladder—Anglo-Saxon *gealla*, bile.

ganglion gang′ glih unn; pl. **ganglia** gang′ glih uh—a group of nerve cell bodies located outside the central nervous system, usually as an enlargement on a nerve.

ganglion nodosum—see **posterior ganglion of vagus nerve.**

gastrocnemius muscle gas trock nee′ mih uss—G. *gastroknemia*, the calf of the leg, from *gastro*, stomach or belly, + *kneme*, the lower leg. Galen called the tibia the "cneme" (Jayne).

gastrolienal ligament gass troh lai′ ee nal—NA, BNA, gastrosplenic, BNA, gastrosplenic omentum, gastrolienal omentum.

geniculate ganglion jeh nick′ iu layt—NA, BNA, genu of facial nerve, BR. L. dim. of *genu*, knee. Ganglion on the facial nerve at the point where the nerve makes a sharp bend.

genital artery—see **gonadal artery.**

genital vein—see **gonadal vein.**

glans penis glannz pee′ niss—L. acorn; somewhat acorn-shaped in man.

glenoid cavity glee′ noyd (fossa)—NA, BNA. G. *glene*, socket of a flat-type joint.

glossopharyngeal nerve gloss oh fuh rinn′ jeh al; gloss oh far inn jee′ al—G. *glossa*, tongue and pharynx. Cranial nerve IX.

glottis—G. *glossa, glotta*, tongue. Opening between pharynx and larynx.

gluteus muscle gloo tee′ uss—G. *gloutas*, rump.

gonadal artery gonn′ add al—genital artery, either ovarian or testicular artery.

gonadal vein—genital vein, either ovarian or testicular vein.

gracilis muscle grass′ ih liss—L. *gracilis*, slender, thin.

gray substance of nervous system—NA, BNA, gray matter of nervous system. Contains nerve cell bodies.

great cutaneous muscle—cutaneous maximus, panniculus carnosus. Not found in man, except as variant anomalies, one of which is called the sternalis muscle.

groin—the ventral region of junction of the thigh with the trunk.

gut—Anglo-Saxon *guttas*, intestine. Used embryologically to denote entire alimentary canal, and often used by zoologists for adult entire alimentary canal.

gyrus jai′ russ; pl. **gyri** jai′ rai—G. *gyros*, a circle. A convolution or fold of the cerebral cortex bounded by fissures or sulci.

hamate bone hay′ mayt—NA, BNA, os hamatum, BNA, unciform bone, OT. L. *hamatus*, from *hamus*, hook, hooked. L. *uncus*, a hook.

hamulus of pterygoid process of postsphenoid bone ham′ iu luss—L. dim. of *hamus*, hook; a little hook.

hemal process hee′ mall—hypapophysis. In lower vertebrates they unite into a hemal arch and surround the caudal artery and vein. Some think the chevron bones are derived from hemal arches.

hepatic sinusoids heh patt′ ick sai′ nuss oyds—capillaries which are slightly larger than typical capillaries, and are lined with modified endothelial cells, some of which are markedly phagocytic.

hepatorenal ligament hepp′ uh toh ree′ nal.

homologous hoh moll′ oh guss—G. *homos*, the same, + *logos*, speech. Corresponding in type of structure.

humerus, greater tubercle hiu′ merr uss—NA, BNA, greater tuberosity, BR.

humerus, lesser tubercle—NA, BNA, lesser tuberosity, BR.

humerus, radial fossa—articular surface for the head of the radius.

hyoid bone hai′ oyd—G. *hyoeides*, the letter upsilon (υ) + *eidos*, form; shaped like the letter υ.

hyoid bone, anterior horn—cranial horn, homologue of the lesser horn of the hyoid bone in man, though actually the larger in most mammals except man.

hyoid bone, posterior horn—caudal cornu, homologue of the greater horn of the hyoid bone in man.

hypo—G. *hypo*, under, beneath; a combining form.

hypoglossal canal hai poh gloss′ al—NA, BNA, anterior condyloid canal, BR, anterior condyloid foramen, OT G. *hypo*, under, + *glossa*, tongue. For the hypoglossal nerve.

hypoglossal nerve—G. *hypo*, under, + *glossa*, tongue. Cranial nerve XII.

hypophyseal fossa hai poh fizz′ eh al—the cavity in the sella turcica of the postsphenoid bone; contains the hypophysis cerebri.

hypophysis cerebri hai poff′ ih sis—NA, BNA, pituitary body, pituitary gland, OT. G. *hypo*, under, + *physis*, growth; an undergrowth.

ileocolic junction ill eh oh koll′ ick—ileocecal, ileocaecal. Guarded by the ileocolic or ileocecal valve (valvuli coli BNA), which is little more than a sphincter muscle protruding into the colon.

ileum ill′ eh umm—L. *ile, ileum, ilium*, groin, flank. Terminal portion of the small intestine, but same derivation as the bone ilium.

iliopsoas muscle ill ih oh soh′ ass; ill ih opp′ soh ass—L. *ilium* + G. *psoa*, a muscle of the loin. Composed of two parts in man, iliacus and psoas.

ilium ill′ ih umm—L. *ile, ileum, ilium*, groin, flank. The long dorsal portion of the os coxa between the sacrum and acetabulum.

incisive foramen inn sai′ sivv—NA, BNA, anterior palatine foramen. Foramen for the nasopalatine vessels and nerve, which is a branch of the maxillary division of the trigeminal nerve.

infra—L. below in position; a combining form.

infraorbital foramen inn fruh orr′ bih tal—for infraorbital branch of the maxillary division of the trigeminal nerve.

infraspinatus muscle inn fruh spai nay′ tuss—located "below" spine of scapula in infraspinatus fossa.

infundibulum of brain inn fun dibb′ iu lumm—NA, infundibulum hypothalamium, BNA, L. a funnel. A funnel-shaped extension of the third ventricle to which the hypophysis cerebri is attached.

infundibulum of uterine tube—NA, infundibulum tubae uterinae, BNA, oviducal funnel. OT.

inguinal ring, deep ing' gwih nal—NA, annulus inguinalis abdominalis, BNA, BR, internal abdominal ring. OT.

inguinal ring, superficial—NA, BR, annulus inguinalis subcutaneous, BNA, external inguinal ring, OT.

innominate artery—see **brachiocephalic artery.**

insertion—originally this term referred to the distal end of an appendicular muscle. The trunk muscles were said to have their origin at the "center" of the trunk, and the insertion was the end of the muscle away from the center. Since this led to considerable confusion in applying the term, it now refers to function rather than to position.

integument inn tegg' iu mennt—L. *integere,* to cover. Any enveloping or covering layer; in anatomy it is the skin and derivitives.

internal abdominal oblique muscle obb leek'; obb laik'—NA, BNA, obliquus abdominis internus, INA.

internal acoustic meatus meh ay' tuss—NA, BNA, internal auditory meatus, BR.

internal iliac artery—NA, BR, NK, OT, hypogastric, BNA.

internal iliac vein—NA, BR, NK, OT, hypogastric, BNA, Parallels internal iliac artery, and joins with external iliac vein to form the common iliac vein.

internal uterine orifice—NA, BNA, os uteri internum, BR, internal os uteri, orificium internum isthmi, NK.

interparietal bone inn terr puh rai' eh tal—occurs occasionally in man and called Inca bone because it is frequently found in Peruvian mummies.

intertubercular groove—NA, BNA, bicipital groove, BR. So named because the tendon of the biceps brachii muscle lies here between the greater and lesser tubercles of the humerus.

ischiocavernosus muscle iss kih oh kavv err noh' suss—NA, BNA, erector penis, OT.

ischium iss' kih umm; pl. **ischia** iss' kih uh—G. *ischion,* hip joint, from *ischein,* to support. Galen introduced the word for the bone which supports the body when seated.

jejunum jeh joo' numm—L. *jejunus,* empty. So called because it was formerly believed to be empty after death.

jugular jugg' iu lerr; joo' giu lerr—L. *jugulum,* the collarbone; akin to L. *jungere,* to yoke, join.

jugular foramen—for a vein and the glossopharyngeal, vagus and accessory nerves.

jugular ganglion—see **anterior ganglion of vagus nerve.**

kidney—Middle English *kidenei,* origin unknown. Latin root is *ren,* Greek root is *nephros.*

lacrimal lack' rih mal—NA, lachrymal, OT.

lacrimal canal—see **nasolacrimal canal.**

lactation lack tay' shunn—L. *lac, lactis,* milk. The secretion of milk from the mammary gland.

lambdoidal lamm' doyd al—like the Greek letter lambda (λ).

lamina lamm' ih nuh; pl. **laminae** lamm' ih nee—L. *lamar,* hinge; a thin plate or scale. In a vertebra the part of the vertebral arch extending from the pedicle to the median plane.

lamina terminalis terr mih nay' liss—NA, BNA, terminal plate, lamina cincercea. Thin sheet at anterior end of third ventricle; it marks anterior end of neural tube of fetus.

laryngeal lah rinn' jeh al; lar inn jee' al.

larynx lar' ingks—G. *larynx.* Taken over into Latin and first used in English in 1578.

lateral circumflex femoral artery—NA, BNA, arteria circumflexa femoris fibularis, INA, circumflexa femoris externa, OT, external circumflex artery.

lateral malleolus mah lee' oh luss—NA, BNA, external malleolus, OT. L. dim. of *malleus,* hammer; little hammer.

lateral thoracic artery—NA, arteria thoracalis lateralis, BNA, long thoracic artery, external mammary artery.

lateral thoracic vein—NA, BNA, long thoracic vein, OT.

latissimus dorsi muscle luh tiss' ih muss dor' sai—L. broadest muscle of the back.

left gastric artery—NA, gastrica sinistra, BNA, coronary artery, OT.

lesser peritoneal sac—NA, BR, omental bursa, BNA, lesser peritoneal cavity.

levator scapulae muscle leh vay' terr, -tor skapp' iu lee—NA, BNA, levator anguli scapulae.

levator scapulae dorsalis muscle—occipitoscapularis, rhomboideus capitis. Supposedly homologous to part of the human rhomboideus muscles.

levator scapulae ventralis muscle—levator scapulae major, levator claviculae.

ligament—L. *ligare,* to bind. A tough band of fibrous connective tissue serving to connect, support, or retain an organ in place.

ligamentum teres ligg uh menn' tumm tee' reez—L. *teres,* rounded, smooth. A round ligament found as round ligament of femur, liver, or uterus.

linea alba linn' eh uh al' buh—L. white line. The median raphe on the abdomen which separates muscles of the right and left sides of the abdominal wall.

liver, ligamentum teres—NA, ligamentum teres hepatis, BNA. In edge of falciform ligament. It represents the obliterated umbilical vein of the fetus.

long thoracic nerve—NA, nervus thoracalis longus, BNA, nerve to serratus anterior, BR, posterior thoracic nerve, dorsal thoracic nerve, external respiratory nerve, OT.

lumbar lumm' berr—L. *lumbus,* loin.

lumbar aponeurosis app oh niu roh' sis—the outer layer of the thoracolumbalis fascia.

lumbodorsal fascia—see **thoracolumbalis fascia.**

lunate bone liu' nayt—NA, os lunatum, BNA, semilunar bone, OT, os intermedium, NK, the intermedium. L. *lunatus,* crescent-shaped, from *luna,* moon.

lunate surface—BNA, articular surface of acetabulum, BR.

lymph limmf—L. *lympha* for earlier *limpa, lumpa,* water, goddess of water, + G. *nymphe,* goddess of moisture. Fluid in lymphatic vessels.

lymph node—lymph gland. Organized collections of lymphatic tissue interposed in the lymphatic stream. These nodes contain masses of lymphocytes produced in the gland and also contain cells of the reticuloendothelial system which ingest foreign particles and debris floating past them in the lymphatic stream.

malleolus mah lee' oh luss—L. dim of *malleus,* hammer.

mammillary mamm' ih lerr ih—L. *mamilla,* dim. of *mamma,* a breast.

mammillary body—terminal of the anterior pillar of the fornix

mammillary process—metapophysis.

mandible—NA, BNA, inferior maxillary bone, inferior maxilla, OT.

mandibular foramen mann dibb' iu leer—NA, BNA, inferior dental foramen, OT.

mandibular fossa—NA, BNA, articular fossa, BR.

manubrium muh niu' brih umm—presternum. L. *manus,* hand; a handle-like part.

manus may' nuss—anterior foot, forefoot, hand. L. *manus,* the hand. Carpals, metacarpals, and digits.

masseter muscle mah see' terr—G. *maseter,* chewer. Origin from zygomatic arch; insertion into mandible; acts as powerful elevator of the mandible.

mastoid process mass' toyd—quite small in the cat.

maxilla mack sill' uh—NA, BNA, maxillary bone, superior maxilla, OT, superior maxillary bone, supramaxilla, OT.

maxillary sinus—NA, BNA, antrum of Highmore, OT. Not present in the cat.

medial malleolus—NA, BNA, internal malleolus, OT.

medulla oblongata meh dull' uh obb long gay' tuh; gah' tuh—L. marrow, pith, + oblong.

medullary velum, anterior medd' uh lerr ih; meh dull' uh rih vee' lumm—NA, BNA, superior medullary velum, BR. L. *velum,* a veil. A thin, medial covering layer of white nervous tissue over the fourth ventricle.

medullary velum, posterior—NA, BNA, inferior medullary velum, BR.

membrane bone—developed in a membrane, never from cartilage; sometimes called dermal bone; presumed by some to be derived from bases of placoid scales which have sunk below the skin in the evolutionary process; thought by others to be derived from dermal bones of fossil armored fish.

meninges meh ninn' jeez; sing. **meninx** mee' ningks—G. *meninx, meningos,* membrane. Membranes covering brain and spinal cord.

mental foramen—two or even three mental foramina may occur in each half of the mandible of some cats.

mesencephalon mess enn seff' uh lonn—midbrain.

mesentery proper mess enn terr ih—mesenterium commune, BNA.

metacarpal bone—G. *meta,* beyond + *karpos,* the wrist; a bone of the metacarpus forefoot (or hand).

metapophysis mett uh poff' ih sis—see **mammillary process.**

metatarsal bone—G. *meta,* after, + *tarsos,* the flat of the foot; a bone of the metatarsus or hindfoot.

metencephalon mett enn seff' uh lonn—G. *meta,* after, + *enkephalos,* brain, from *in* + *kephale,* head; afterbrain. The term afterbrain is also often used for the myelencephalon.

middle cerebellar peduncle—NA, BR, brachium pontis, BNA, crus ponto-cerebellare, NK. L. *brachium,* arm, + *pons,* bridge.

middle ear—the narrow cavity in the temporal bone between the tympanic membrane and the inner ear. Embryologically derived from the first pharyngeal pouch, which later encloses the auditory ossicles, the malleus, incus and stapes.

middle nasal concha—NA, BNA, middle turbinal, ethmoturbinal, OT.

middle rectal vein—NA, middle hemorrhoidal vein; parallels middle rectal artery.

middle sacral artery—continuation of the aorta; may be called the caudal artery in the tail.

middle sacral vein—parallels middle sacral artery; arises as the caudal vein; usually empties into the left common iliac vein, but may enter right common iliac vein or show considerable variation.

molar—L. *molaris,* from *mola,* mill; a tooth adapted for grinding.

muscle—L. *musculus,* dim. of *mus,* mouse, because of the supposed resemblance of the contraction of a muscle to the movement of a mouse under a cloth.

muscular vein—parallels muscular artery.

myelencephalon mai eh lenn seff' uh lonn—afterbrain, spinal brain, OT. G. *myelos,* marrow; now often applied to spinal cord; therefore, the part of the brain nearest the spinal cord.

myelin sheath mai' eh linn—medullary sheath, sheath of Schwann, OT. White sheath around certain nerve fibers, nonliving, and composed mostly of lipoidal material.

naris nay' riss; pl. **nares** nay' rees—NA, BNA, anterior naris, external naris, OT, nostrils. External opening of entire nose; see **anterior nasal aperture.**

nasolacrimal canal nay zoh lack' rih mal—NA, BNA, lacrimal canal, lachrymal canal, nasal canal, OT.

nasopharynx nay zoh far' ingks—nasal portion of the pharynx.

navicular bone nuh vick' iu lerr—NA, os naviculare pedis, BNA, BR, os centrale tarsi, NK, scaphoid bone, scaphoid, centrale of foot, OT. (Also BNA for the scaphoid of the hand.)

nerve—a collection of nerve cell processes held together by connective tissue; it never includes the cell bodies.

nerve fiber—a process of a neuron.

neural arch—see **vertebral arch.**

neural tube—formed by the union of the ectodermal neural folds in early embryological development and gives rise to the brain and spinal cord.

neuron niu' rohn—neurone. A nerve cell, consisting of cell body and all of its processes.

notochord noh' toh kord—chorda dorsalis. G. *notos,* back, + *chorde,* string. A longitudinal rod of elastic cells lying dorsal to the intestine and ventral to the neural tube. In vertebrates it is surrounded and partially or entirely replaced by the centrum of the vertebrae.

obturator foramen obb' tiu ray terr—NA, BNA, thyroid foramen, OT. L. *obturare,* to stop up, or close.

occipital condyles ock sipp' ih tal konn' dills—articulate with the anterior articular surfaces of the atlas, permitting a nodding motion.

odontoid process—see **dens.**

olecranon oh leck' ruh nonn; oh leh kray' nonn—NA, BNA, olecranon process. G. *olene,* elbow, + *cranium,* head; the proximal process of the ulna which forms the point of the elbow.

olecranon fossa—articulating surface on the humerus for the olecranon process of the ulna.

omentum—a mesentery passing from stomach to another abdominal organ or to the body wall.

omentum, greater—NA, omentum majus, BNA, great omentum, gastrocolic omentum, OT.

omentum, lesser—NA, omentum minus, BNA, gastrohepatic omentum, OT.

ophthalmic nerve off thal' mick—G. *opthalmos,* eye. Division of trigeminal nerve, NA, to the region of orbit.

optic canal (foramen)—for the passage of the optic nerve.

optic chiasma kai azz' muh—G. two lines placed crosswise like the letter chi (χ).

optic groove—see **chiasmatic groove.**

orbital fissure fish' err; fish' iur—NA, fissura orbitalis superior, BNA, superior orbital fissure, sphenoidal fissure, OT, foramen lacerum anterior, OT. For a branch of the carotid artery, which goes to the cranial cavity; the oculomotor, trochlear, and abducens nerves; and the ophthalmic division of the trigeminal nerve.

organ of Corti—see **spiral organ.**

origin—in the earlier definitions, origin of an appendicular muscle referred to the proximal end, and the origin of a trunk muscle had reference to the "central" end as discussed under **insertion.** Now it refers to the relatively immovable end; it never referred to its embryological beginning.

os ahs; pl. **ossa** ahs' uh; gen. *ossis*—L. bone.

os ahs; pl. **ora** oh' ruh; gen. *oris*—L. mouth.

os coxa ahs kock suh; pl. **ossa coxae** ahs' uh kock' see—NA, BNA, innominate bone, hipbone, OT.

ossicle ahs' ih kehl—L. *ossiculum,* dim. of **os,** bone; a small bone.

ovarian follicle—NA, BR, vesicular ovarian follicle, BNA, Graafian follicle, vesicular follicle, OT.

palatine bone, horizontal portion pal' uh tine; -tinn—NA, pars horizontalis, BNA, horizontal lamina or plate, BR, palatal lamina, NK, INA.

palatine bone, perpendicular portion—NA, pars perpendicularis, BNA, perpendicular lamina or plate, BR, maxillary lamina, NK, INA, vertical portion, nasal portion, OT.

pallium pal' ih umm—L. a cloak.

pancreas pann' kreh uss; panng' kreh uss—G. *pan,* all, + *kreas,* flesh; from the nature of sweetbreads as eaten.

pancreatic duct pann kreh att' ick; panng kreh att' ick—NA, BNA, duct of Wirsung, canal of Wirsung, OT.

papilla puh pill' uh—L. nipple; nipple-like.

papillary muscle papp' ih lerr ih; puh pill' uh rih—NA, BNA. Muscular projections from the walls of the ventricles of the heart to which chordae tendinae are attached.

parasympathetic nervous system—NA, craniosacral division of nervous system, BNA.

parietal puh rai' eh tal—L. *paries,* a wall; pertaining to a wall.

parotid duct puh rott' idd—NA, BNA, Stensen's duct, Steno's duct, duct of Steno, Stenon's duct, OT.

parotid duct, orifice of—found on inside of cheek opposite the most prominent cusp of the last premolar tooth.

parotid gland—G. *para,* beside, + *ous, otos,* ear.

patella bone puh tell' uh—NA, BNA, kneepan, kneecap. L. a small pan, dim. of *patina,* pan. A sesamoid bone developed in the tendon of the quadriceps femoris muscle.

pectinate muscle—musculi pectinati, L. *pecten,* a comb. One of a number of muscular columns that line the auricles of the atria of the heart.

pectineus muscle peck tinn' eh uss; peck tih nee' uss.

pectoantebrachialis muscle peck toh ann teh bray kih ay' liss; -brack ih ay' liss—often spelled pectoantibrachialis but contrary to its derivation; see **antebrachium.**

pectoral—L. breast.

pectoral girdle—consists typically of a dorsal scapula and a ventral corocoid and/or a precoracoid. In mammals the corocoids are reduced to a coracoid process except in the monotremes.

pectoralis major muscle pecktoh ray' liss—ectopectoralis, OT.

pectoralis minor muscle—entopectoralis, OT.

pedicle pedd' ih kehl—NA, BR, radix, BNA. L. *pediculus,* little foot. In a vertebra it is the basal part of each side of the vertebral arch connecting the laminae with the body.

peduncle peh dunng' kehl—L. *pes,* foot, + dim. *-culus;* little foot.

pelvis—greater or major pelvis, NA, BNA, false pelvis, BR; lesser or minor pelvis, NA, BNA, true pelvis, BR. L. a basin.

penis pee' niss—L. male copulatory organ.

perforated substance of brain, anterior and **posterior**—a layer of gray substance in which there are numerous small apertures through which small blood vessels pass.

peritoneum perr ih toh nee' umm—G. *peritonaion,* from *peritonos,* stretched around or over.

peroneal muscle perr oh nee' al—G. *perone,* a pin, hence the fibula. Near the fibula.

pes peez; pl. **pedes** pee' deez; pedd' eez—posterior foot, hind foot. The tarsal bones, metatarsal bones, and digits.

phalanx fay langks; fal' angks; pl. **phalanges** fah lann' jeez—proximal, middle, distal, NA, BR, first, second, third pha-

phalanx—continued
lanx, BNA. G. *phalanx,* soldiers in close order. One of the bones of a digit, a finger or toe.

pharynx far' ingks—G. throat.

phrenic freen' ick—G. *phren,* diaphragm; of or pertaining to the diaphragm.

pia mater, pai' uh may' ter—L. *pia,* tender, kind, + *mater,* mother.

pineal body pinn' eh al—NA, BNA, pineal gland, epiphysis cerebri, epiphysis. L. *pinea,* the cone of a pine.

piriform area pirr' ih form—pyriform lobe, NA, BNA, tractus postrhinalis. L. *pirum,* pear, + *forma,* form. Relatively small in man; part of the archipallium.

pisiform bone pai' sih form—postminimus. L. *pisum,* pea, + *forma,* form. Usually considered to be a sesamoid bone developed in the tendon of the flexor carpi ulnaris muscle, though regarded by some as part of an elementary digit; the bone of the proximal row of carpal bones.

pituitary gland—see **hypophysis cerebri**

plantaris muscle plann tay' riss—L. *planta,* the sole of the foot.

platysma muscle pluh tizz' muh—NA, BNA, platysma myoides, tetragonus, OT. G. *platysma,* flat plate.

pleura plur' uh—G. a rib, the side.

pons—NA, BNA, pons Varolii, pons cerebelli, OT. L. a bridge.

popliteus muscle popp litt' eh uss; popp lih tee' uss—L. *poples,* ham. Pertaining to the ham, or back part of leg below the knee.

portal vein—NA, BNA, hepatic portal vein. L. *porta,* gate. So named because it enters the porta hepatis or gate of the liver. The term hepatic is omitted in mammals because they have no renal portal vein. A portal vein takes blood from capillaries to a second set of capillaries.

posterior articular process—caudal articular process, NK, inferior articular process, BNA, postzygapophysis, OT.

posterior articular surface—inferior articular facet or surface, BNA, inferior articular surface, BR.

posterior cerebellar peduncle—NA, restiform body, BNA, inferior cerebellar peduncle, BR, crus medullocerebellare, NK. L. *restus,* rope, + *forma,* like; a ropelike body.

posterior cervical ganglion—inferior cervical ganglion, BNA.

posterior commissure komm' ih shur; komm' iss ur—commisura posterior cerebri, BNA. A thin band of white fibers crossing between the anterior colliculi.

posterior epigastric artery and vein—inferior epigastric, BNA, deep epigastric, OT.

posterior ganglion of vagus nerve—NA, nodosum, BNA, inferior ganglion, BR. L. *nodosus,* from *nodus,* knot. Large ganglion of the vagus distal to the jugular foramen.

posterior gluteal artery and vein—inferior gluteal, BNA, ischiatic, sciatic, OT.

posterior mesenteric artery and vein—inferior mesenteric, BNA, caudal mesenteric, INA.

posterior mesenteric ganglion—inferior mesenteric ganglion, BNA. In the cat it may be either single or double, is quite

small, and is located on the posterior mesenteric artery, about ½–¼ inch from its origin from the aorta.

posterior nasal aperture—NA, BNA, posterior bony aperture of the nose, BR, posterior naris, internal naris, OT. See also **choane.**

posterior palatine canal—for the descending palatine artery and the palatine branch of the maxillary division of the trigeminal nerve.

posterior vena cava—inferior vena cava, BNA, caudal vena cava, NK, ascending vena cava, postcava, postcaval vein, OT.

postsphenoid bone post sfee' noyd—posterior sphenoid bone, basisphenoid, OT. In the cat it is sometimes called the sphenoid without any modifying term; basisphenoid should apply only to the body of the postsphenoid bone.

postsphenoid bone, body—basisphenoid.

postsphenoid bone, great wing—NA, BNA, alisphenoid, OT.

postzygapophysis—see **posterior articular process.**

premaxilla pree macks ill' uh—incisive bone, BNA. Usually fused with the maxilla in man.

premaxilla, nasal process—frontal process, BNA, since it is a part of the frontal process of the maxilla in man.

premolar—deciduous molar, BNA.

prepuce pree' pius—L. *praeputium,* foreskin of penis.

presphenoid bone—in the cat consists of the median presphenoid proper and two orbitosphenoids.

presphenoid bone, small wing—orbitosphenoid.

prezygapophysis—see **anterior articular process.**

pronation pro nay' shunn—L. *pronare,* to bend forward to the prone position. A medial rotation of the hand and radius around the ulna, so that the palm is turned downward or toward the back. Opposed to supination.

pronator teres muscle pro nay' tor tee' reez—NA, BNA, pronator radii teres, OT. L. a round pronator muscle.

prosencephalon prahs enn seff' uh lonn—forebrain. G. *pros,* toward, + *encephalon,* brain.

prostate gland prahs' tayt—G. *prostates,* one who stands before, a guard or protector.

proximal prock' sih mal—that end nearest to the midline of the body. Opposed to distal.

psoas muscle soh' ass; psoh' ass—G. muscle of the loin.

pterygoid process terr' ih goyd;—G. ptero-, pter-, from *pteron,* feather, wing; winglike.

pubis piu' biss; pl. **pubes** piu' bezz—L. *pubes,* adult.

pulmonary valve—valve of pulmonary trunk.

pylorus pai loh' russ; pih loh' russ—NA, BNA, pyloric orifice, G. *pylorus,* gatekeeper.

quadriceps femoris muscle kwodd' rih sepps femm' oh riss—NA, BNA, quadriceps extensor femoris, quadriceps extensor, OT.

radial nerve—NA, BNA, musculospiral nerve, OT.

radius—L. a staff, rod, spoke of a wheel.

radius, head—NA, caput, BNA, capitellum, BR.

radius, tuberosity—NA, BNA, radial tubercle, INA, bicipital tuberosity. It is the point for insertion of the biceps brachii muscle.

ramus ray' muss; pl. **rami** ray' mai—L. a branch. Usually used for the branch of a nerve.

raphe ray' fee—G. *raphe,* a seam or suture, from *rhaphtein,* to sew or stitch together. The line of union of two similar structures.

rectum—L. *rectus,* straight. Named by Galen because he found it straight in lower animals.

rectus abdominis muscle abb domm' ih niss—literally, straight of the abdomen; when the muscle contracts, it straightens the abdominal wall.

rectus femoris muscle—literally, straight of the femur; it acts to straighten the tibia in line with the femur.

renal ree' nal—L. *ren,* kidney; pertaining to the kidney.

restiform body—see **posterior cerebellar peduncle.**

retroperitoneal ree troh perr ih toh nee' al; rett roh perr ih toh nee' al—L. *retro,* behind; behind the peritoneum.

rhombencephalon romm benn seff' uh lonn—hindbrain. A rhomboid-shaped structure in some embryos.

rhomboideus muscle romm' boyde us—rhomboid.

rostrum ross' trumm—L. a beak.

saccule sack' iul—L. *saccus,* bag, + dim. -ulus; a little sac. An organ of equilibrium because it contains hair cells, which are stimulated by the position of the head.

sacrum say' krumm—L. *sacer,* sacred. This bone was thought to survive and form part of the body after resurrection. Consists of three fused sacral vertebrae in the cat.

saphenous suh fee' nuss—L. *saphena,* a vein in the leg, from G. *saphenes,* clear or manifest, or Arabic *al-safin,* hidden.

saphenous artery—smaller and less important in man than in the cat.

saphenous nerve—NA, BNA, long saphenous nerve, internal saphenous nerve.

saphenous vein—large saphenous vein, BNA, long saphenous vein, OT, internal saphenous vein, OT.

sartorius muscle sar toh' rih uss—L. *sartor,* a tailor. Muscle used in rotating the leg to the tailor's sitting position.

scalenus skay lee' nuss—G. *skalenos,* uneven.

scalenus dorsalis muscle—scalenus posterior, BNA, scalenus posticus, OT.

scalenus ventralis muscle—scalenus anterior, BNA, scalenus anticus, OT.

scaphoid bone skaff' oyd—NA, BR, navicular bone, os naviculare manus, BNA, radiale. G. *skaphe,* boat, + *eidos,* form; boatlike. Also OT for the navicular bone of the foot.

scapholunar bone skaff oh liu' nerr—BR, type form, naviculolunate bone, BNA, type form. A fusion of the scaphoid bone with the lunate bone.

scapula skapp' iu luh—G. *skaptein,* to dig; because the bone was thought to resemble a spade.

scapula, anterior border—BR, cranial border, INA, superior border, BNA, coracoid border.

scapula, coracoid process—ossifies separately as an atavistic epiphysis for the coracoid, precoracoid, or both.

scapula, lateral border—NA, axillary border, BNA, caudal border, glenoid border.

scapula, medial border—NA, BR, vertebral border, BNA.

scapula, spine—NA, BNA, crest, BR.

sciatic nerve sai att' ick—NA, BNA, great sciatic nerve. L. *sciaticus,* from L. *ischiadicus,* from *ischium.*

scrotum skroh' tumm—perhaps from L. *scortum,* leather.

sella turcica sell' uh terr' sih kuh—L. Turkish saddle, because of its resemblance to the shape of high-backed Turkish saddles. The cavity in the sella turcica is the hypophyseal fossa for the hypophysis.

semicircular canals, posterior, superior, and **lateral**—NA, BNA. Cavities in the petrous portion of the temporal bone, which contain the semicircular ducts.

semicircular ducts, posterior, superior, and **lateral**—NA, BNA. Parts of the membranous labyrinth of the ear located in the semicircular canals. They connect with the utricle, and each has an ampulla on one end containing hair cells, which are stimulated by movements of the contained endolymph.

semilunar ganglion—see **trigeminal ganglion.**

semimembranosus muscle semm ih memm bruh noh' sus—L. *semi,* half, + *membrana,* membrane. In man this muscle is part muscle and part a tough connective tissue membrane.

semitendinosus muscle semm ih tenn dih noh' sus—L. *semi,* half, + *tendo,* tendon. In man this muscle is part muscle and part tendon.

septum pellucidum sepp' tumm peh liu' sih dumm—NA, BNA, transparent septum, septum lucidum, BR, OT. L. *saeptum,* a fence, + *per,* through, + *lucere,* to shine. Two thin sheets forming medial boundaries of the lateral ventricles which enclose a small space.

serous membrane—serosa. A thin membrane consisting of flat mesothelial cells on a connective tissue base and lining a closed cavity, either the celom or a cavity derived from it.

serrate serr' ayt—L. *serratus,* notched, from *serra,* a saw.

serratus dorsalis anterior muscle—serratus posterior superior, BNA, serratus dorsalis cranialis, INA.

serratus dorsalis posterior muscle seh ray' tuss dor say' liss—serratus posterior inferior, BNA, serratus dorsalis caudalis, INA.

serratus ventralis muscle venn tray' liss—serratus anterior, BNA, serratus lateralis, INA, serratus magnus, OT.

sinus venosus sai' nuss veh noh' sus—chamber of the heart in lower vertebrates and embryos of higher forms, which receives large veins and empties into the right atrium. In adult mammals it becomes the part of the right atrium between the anterior and posterior venae cavae.

skull—Anglo Saxon *skulle,* a bowl. Variously defined as the cranium; the cranium and bones of face; the cranium, face, and lower jaw; the cranium, face, lower jaw, hyoid, and auditory ossicles.

soleus muscle soh' leh uss—L. *solea,* a sole of a shoe, a sandal. The muscle in man is flat and thin like a shoe sole.

sphenoid sfee' noyd—G. *sphen,* a wedge, + *eidos,* form; wedge-shaped.

sphenoid, great wing—NA, BNA, alisphenoidal region, wing of postsphenoid.

sphenoid, small wing—NA, BNA, orbitosphenoidal region, wing of presphenoid.

sphenopalatine foramen sfee' noh pal' uh tine; -tinn—for the sphenopalatine artery and the pterygopalatine branch of the maxillary division of the trigeminal nerve.

sphincter muscle sfingk' terr—G. *sphinkter,* a band, from *sphingein,* to bind. A ringlike muscle surrounding an opening.

spinal cord—NA, BR, medulla spinalis, BNA.

spinal ganglion—NA, BNA, posterior root ganglion, dorsal root ganglion.

spinodeltoideus muscle—spinodeltoid.

spinotrapezius muscle—trapezius inferior.

spinous process spai' nuss—NA, BNA, neural spine, OT.

spiral ganglion of the cochlea—NA, BNA, ganglion of Corti, OT. Located on vestibulocochlear nerve and receives fibers from the spiral organ (organ of Corti) in cochlear duct of the ear.

spiral organ—NA, organ of Corti, BNA.

splanchnic splangk' nick—G. *splanchna,* the viscera; pertaining to the viscera.

splenium splee' nih umm—G. *splenion,* a bandage. A structure resembling a bandaged part.

squamous skway' muss—L. *squama,* a scale; resembling a scale.

stellate ganglion stell' ayt—cervicothoracic ganglion. L. *stellatus,* from *stella,* star; star-shaped. The posterior cervical fused with the first three thoracic in the cat; in other mammals often fused with only the first thoracic.

sternebra sterr' neh bruh; pl. **sternebrae** sterr' neh bree—G. *sternon,* breastbone; L. *vertebra,* joint. Bony segments of the sternum.

sternum sterr' numm—G. *sternon,* the breast, chest. Consists of three regions in the cat; presternum or manubrium, mesosternum or body and metasternum or xiphoid process.

sternum, body—mesosternum, gladiolus, OT. L. *gladiolus,* a small sword.

styliform process of temporal bone stai' lih form—L. *stylus,* a writing instrument, from G. *stylos* + *forma,* form. Probably not homologous to the styloid process of man.

stylohyal bone stai loh hai' al—in man it fuses with the tympanohyal to form the distal portion of the styloid process.

styloid process stai' loyd—L. *stylus,* a writing instrument.

stylomastoid foramen stai loh mass' toyd—for exit of the facial nerve.

subclavian subb klay' vih ann—L. *sub,* under, + *clavicle.*

submandibular gland—NA, BR, NK, submaxillary gland, BNA, OT. The mandible used to be called the inferior maxilla.

subscapularis muscle subb skapp iu lay' riss—L. *sub,* under, + scapula.

sulcus sull' kuss; pl. **sulci** sull' sai—L. a furrow. A groove on the surface of the brain, separating gyri.

superficial epigastric vein—parallels superficial epigastric artery.

supination siu pih nay' shunn—L. *supinare,* to turn palm upward or to lie backward. A rotation of the hand and radius around the ulna so that the palm is turned toward the front. Opposed to pronation.

supra—L. *supra,* above; a combining form.

supracondyloid—supracondylar, used almost interchangeably.

suprarenal gland—NA, adrenal gland, BNA.

supraspinatus muscle siu proh spai nay' tuss—L. *supra,* above, + spine; above the spine of the scapula.

suture—L. *sutura,* a seam, from *suere,* to sew. When between bones of the skull, it is between two bones formed in membrane and still separated by connective tissue.

sympathetic ganglia—ganglia of sympathetic trunk, NA, BNA, paravertebral ganglia, vertebral ganglia, central ganglia.

sympathetic nervous system—NA, IANC, thoracolumbar division of autonomic nervous system.

sympathetic trunk—truncus sympathicus, NA, BNA.

symphysis sim' fi sis—a union of two bones by fibrocartilage.

synchondrosis sing konn droh' sis; sinn konn droh' sis—G. *syn,* with, + *chondros,* cartilage, + *-osos,* condition. A connection between two bones being formed in cartilage and therefore united temporarily by hyaline cartilage.

synovial joint sih noh' vih al—G. *syn,* with, + *ovum,* egg; perhaps because of the resemblance of synovial fluid to egg white in consistency. It is a highly specialized joint in which smooth bony surfaces covered with hyaline cartilage come in contact, and which is held in place by a tough capsule lined with a synovial membrane of connective tissue which secretes just enough viscous fluid to keep the surfaces lubricated.

talus tay' luss—NA, BNA astragalus, OT. L. *talus,* a knucklebone used as dice. G. *astragalos,* vertebrae and ankle bones used as dice.

tarsal bones—NA, tarsus. G. *tarsos,* used for a number of objects with flat surfaces, e.g., rudder, basketwork. Galen first used it for the foot but applied it only to the distal bones. In the Middle Ages it was restricted to the back of the foot, as now (Jayne).

tarsale tar say' lee; pl. **tarsalia** tar say' lih uh—one of the distal row of tarsals articulating with a metatarsal.

telencephlon tell enn seff' uh lonn—G. *telos,* end, + *enkephalos,* brain; endbrain.

temporal bone, petrous portion pett' russ; pee' truss—G. *petros,* a stone.

temporal bone, squamous portion skway' muss—L. *squama,* a scale. Its flat edge overlies the parietal bone like a fish scale.

tendo calcaneus—NA, BNA, tendo musculus tricipitis surae, INA, tendon of Achilles, OT, heel tendon.

tendon—L. *tendo,* from *tendere,* to stretch, after G. *tenon, teinein,* to stretch. Tendons are continuous with the connective tissue sheaths of the muscle and when inserted into a bone, with the periosteum of the bone.

tensor fasciae latae muscle tenn′ sor fassh′ ih ee lay′ tee—NA, BNA, tensor vaginae femoris, tensor fasciae femoris.

tentorium of the parietal bone tenn toh′ rih umm—conspicuous in the cat, but not present in man. It divides the cerebellum from the cerebral hemispheres and is similar in position to the tentorium cerebelli of the dura mater of man.

tenuissimus muscle tenn iu iss′ ih muss—abductor cruris. L. *tenuis,* thin; superlatively thin.

teres tee reez—L. round or smooth.

teres major muscle—the greater round muscle.

teres minor muscle—the smaller round muscle.

thalamus thal′ uh muss—optic thalamus, OT. G. *thalamos,* an inner chamber. An important sensory center on path to cerebral cortex.

thalamus, intermediate mass—massa intermedia, NA, BNA, gray, middle, or soft commissure, medicommissure.

thoracic thoh rass′ ick—G. *thorax, thorakos,* chest; pertaining to the chest.

thoracodorsal nerve thoh′ ruh koh dor′ sal; thoh ray′ koh—NA, BNA, nerve to latissimus dorsi, BR, long subscapular nerve.

thoracolumbalis fascia—NA, lumbodorsal fascia, lumbar fascia. Its outer layer is called the lumbar aponeurosis.

thoracolumbar division of the autonomic system—see **sympathetic nervous system.**

thyrohyal bone—a bone of the posterior horn of the hyoid bone of the cat which attaches to the thyroid cartilage of the larynx. This horn corresponds to the greater horn of the human hyoid bone.

tibia tibb′ ih uh—L. an ancient flute fashioned from a leg bone. Celsus used it first; Galen called it the "cneme"; and the Germans called it the skin bone, therefore our term, the shin bone (Jayne). The larger of the two bones of the lower leg.

tibia, intercondylar eminence—NA, BR, intercondyloid eminence, BNA, spine of tibia, OT, intercondylic, intercondylous. A double ridge of intercondylar tubercles separated by an intercondylar area.

tibia, intercondylar fossa in terr konn′ dih lerr—NA, BR, intercondyloid fossa on tibia, BNA, intercondylic, intercondylous.

tibialis anterior muscle tibb ih ay′ liss ann tee′ rih or—NA, BNA, tibialis anticus, OT.

tibialis posterior muscle tibb ih ay′ liss poss tee′ rih or—NA, BNA, tibialis posticus, OT.

trabeculae carneae truh beck′ iu lee kar′ neh ee—NA, BNA, columnae carneae, OT.

trachea tray′ keh uh—G. *tracheia,* rough. Aristotle called the arteries smooth, and the windpipe a rough artery; a "tracheia arteria"; see **artery.**

transverse foramen—NA, BNA, foramen transversarium, BNA, vertebrarterial foramen, costotransverse foramen.

transverse vein—a conspicuous connection in the cat between the two facial veins.

transversus abdominis muscle tranns verr′ sus abb domm′ ih niss—NA, BNA, transversalis abdominis, OT.

transversus costarum muscle—sternocostalis externus muscle.

trapezium of medulla oblongata—not found in man.

trapezium bone of wrist truh pee′ zih umm—NA, BR, greater multangular bone, BNA, G. *trapezion,* a little table, irregularly four-sided.

trapezius muscle truh pee′ zih uss—NA, BNA, cucullaris, OT.

trapezoid bone of wrist trapp′ eh zoyd—NA, BR, lesser multangular bone, BNA. G. *trapeza,* table, + *eidos,* form. A four-sided figure with two parallel sides.

triangular bone—NA, triquetrum, BNA, cuneiform bone, OT, pyramidal bone, OT, ulnare, NK, L. *triquetrus,* three-cornered.

triceps brachii muscle, lateral head trai′ sepps bray′ kih ai; brack′ ih ai—NA, caput laterale, BNA, external head, OT, anconeus lateralis.

triceps brachii muscle, long head—NA, caput longum, BNA, middle or scapular head, OT, anconeus longus, OT.

triceps brachii muscle, medial head—NA, caput mediale, BNA, internal head, OT, anconeus medialis. Consists of 1—a long portion (anconeus posterior); 2—an intermediate portion (anconeus internus); and 3—a short portion.

triceps surae muscle trai′ sepps siu′ ree—NA, BNA. L. *sura,* calf of the leg. The gastrocnemius and soleus considered as one muscle, since they insert by the tendo calcaneus.

tricuspid valve—see **atrioventricular valve, right.**

trigeminal ganglion—NA, BR, semilunar ganglion, BNA, Gasserian ganglion, OT. L. *semi,* half, + *luna,* moon. Located on afferent root of trigeminal nerve. Also used as OT for celiac ganglion.

trigeminal nerve trai jemm′ ih nal—L. *trigeminus,* born three together; because of the three divisions of the nerve. Cranial Nerve V.

triquetrum—see **triangular bone.**

trochlea trock′ leh uh—G. *trochilia,* the sheaf of a pulley; shaped like a pulley.

trochlear nerve trock′ leh err—NA, BNA, pathetic nerve, OT. Supplies superior oblique muscle, which passes through a fibrocartilaginous pulley in man. Cranial Nerve IV.

tubercle tiu′ berr kehl—L. *tuberculum,* dim. of tuber, knob; a small knoblike prominence; smaller than a tuberosity.

tubercle of a rib—tubercular head of a rib.

tubercle of tibia—NA, BR, tuberosity, BNA.

tuberosity tiu berr oss′ ih tih—L. *tuber,* knob, + *osity,* condition; a prominence, usually larger than a tubercle.

tympanic bulla timm pann′ ick bull′ uh—auditory bulla.

tympanohyal bone timm puh noh hai′ al—a bone of the anterior horn of the hyoid bone which articulates with the tympanic bulla in the cat.

ulna ull′ nuh—L. elbow, forearm, from G. *olene,* elbow.

ulna, trochlear notch—NA, BR, semilunar notch, BNA, greater sigmoid notch, OT. It articulates with the trochlea of the humerus.

umbilical artery umm bill′ ih kal—supplies urinary bladder in cat after birth; was much larger before birth, when it supplied the allantochorion.

ureter iu ree′ ter—duct leading from kidney to urinary bladder, or in lower forms, the cloaca.

urethra iu ree′ thruh—duct leading from urinary bladder to the outside in the male, or to the vestibule in the female.

urinary bladder, suspensory ligament—probably homologous, at least in part, to the median umbilical ligament, NA, of man.

uterine tube iu′ terr inn; -ine—NA, tuba uterina, BNA, Fallopian tube, OT, oviduct, salpinx, OT.

uterus iu′ terr uss—L. womb. That part of the Müllerian tube or embryological oviduct in which the young develop or eggs are stored.

uterus, broad ligament—NA, ligamentum latum uteri, BNA.

uterus, horn—NA, cornu.

uterus, round ligament—NA, ligamentum teres uteri, BNA, chorda uteroinguinalis, INA.

utricle iu′ trih kehl—the part of the membranous labyrinth into which the semicircular ducts open; contains hair cells stimulated by the position of the head.

vagina vuh jai′ nuh—L. a sheath. That portion of the embryonic oviduct which becomes specialized to receive the penis of the male.

vagus nerve vay′ guss—NA, BNA, pneumogastric nerve, OT. L. *vagus,* wandering. Cranial Nerve X.

valve of coronary sinus—NA, BNA, valve of Thebesius, OT, Thebesian valve, OT, coronary valve, OT.

vastus intermedius muscle vass′ tuss in terr mee′ dih uss—NA, BNA, crureus, OT.

vastus lateralis muscle latt eh ray′ liss—NA, BNA, vastus externus, OT, vastus fibularis, INA.

vastus medialis muscle mee dih ay′ liss—NA, BNA, vastus internus, OT, vastus tibialis, INA.

vena cava vee′ nuh kay′ vuh; pl. **venae cavae** vee′ nee kay′ vee—L. *vena,* vein, + *cava,* hollow.

ventral—L. *ventralis,* from *venter,* the belly; abdominal side as opposed to dorsal side.

ventral nasal concha—inferior nasal concha, BNA, inferior turbinal, OT, maxilloturbinal, OT.

ventral primary division of a spinal nerve—NA, ventral ramus, NK, anterior ramus, BNA, BR.

ventral root of a spinal nerve—NA, NK, anterior root, BNA, BR.

vermis of cerebellum verr′ miss—L. worm. Named from a fancied resemblance to a segmented worm.

vertebra verr′ teh bruh; pl. **vertebrae** verr′ teh bree—L. from *vertere,* to turn.

vertebral arch verr′ teh bral—NA, BNA, neural arch, OT. The arch of a vertebra which encloses the spinal cord.

vertebral canal—NA, BNA, spinal canal, neural canal, OT.

vertebral foramen—NA, BNA, spinal foramen, OT.

vertebral notch—NA, incisura vertebralis, BNA, intervertebral notch.

vestibular ganglion—located on the vestibulocochlear nerve which supplies the sense organs of equilibrium in the utricle, saccule, and ampullae of the semicircular ducts.

vestibule of the vagina—NA, vestibulum vaginae, BNA, urogenital sinus.

vestibulocochlear nerve—NA, nervus acusticus, BNA, auditory nerve, BR, N. octavus, OT. Cranial nerve VIII.

vestigial vess tihj′ ih al—L. *vestigium,* a footprint. Pertaining to a small, degenerate, or imperfectly developed part, which presumably has been more fully developed in an earlier stage of the individual or in a past generation.

visceral arches viss′ err al—splanchnocranium, visceral skeleton. Supports of cartilage or bone for the gills and jaws of fish, and transitory or modified in embryos of higher forms.

vulva vull′ vuh—L. a covering. The external genitalia of the female, including labia and clitoris.

white substance of the nervous system—NA, BNA, white matter of nervous system. Contains nerve fibers, some of which are myelinated, but never contains cell bodies.

xiphoid process zif′ oid—NA, xiphisternum, BNA, ensiform process, OT, metasternum, OT. G. *xiphos,* sword; L. *ensis,* sword. The most posterior bony element of the sternum.

zygapophysis zai guh poff′ ih sis; zigg uh poff′ ih sis; pl. **zygapophyses** zai guh poff′ ih seez—articular process. G. *zygon,* yoke, + L. *apohysis,* offshoot, process. Called either prezygapophyses or postzygapophyses.

zygomatic zai goh matt′ ick; zigg oh—G. *zygon,* yoke; of, or pertaining to the zygomatic arch.

zygomatic bone—NA, BNA, malar, OT, jugal, OT. G. *zygoma,* to yoke; L. *mala,* cheek; L. *jugalis,* from jugum, yoke.

zygomatic bone, frontal process—NA, BNA, postorbital process, OT.

SELECTED REFERENCES

AREY, LESLIE B. Developmental anatomy. 7th ed. Philadelphia: W. B. Saunders Co., 1965.

BIGELOW, ROBERT P. Directions for the dissection of the cat. 2d ed. New York: Macmillan Co., 1935.

BLOOM, W. and FAWCETT, D. W. A textbook of histology. 9th ed. Philadelphia: W. B. Saunders Co., 1968.

BREMER, J. LEWIS. A textbook of histology. Edited by H. L. WEATHERFORD. 6th ed. Philadelphia: Blakiston Co., 1944.

CUNNINGHAM, DANIEL J. Textbook of anatomy. Edited by G. J. ROMANES. 10th ed. London, New York, Toronto: Oxford University Press, 1964.

DAVISON, ALVIN. Mammalian anatomy, with special reference to the cat. Edited by FRANK A. STROMSTEN. 7th ed. Philadelphia: Blakiston Co., 1947.

GARDNER, ERNEST. Fundamentals of neurology. 4th ed. Philadelphia: W. B. Saunders Co., 1963.

GOODRICH, EDWIN S. Studies on the structure and development of vertebrates. London: Macmillan & Co., 1930.

GRANT, J. C. BOILEAU and BASMAJIAN, J. V. A method of anatomy. 7th ed. Baltimore: Williams & Wilkins Co.: 1965.

———. An atlas of anatomy. 5th ed. Baltimore: Williams & Wilkins Co., 1962.

GRAY, HENRY. Anatomy of the human body. Edited by CHARLES M. GOSS. 28th ed. Philadelphia: Lea & Febiger, 1966.

FLOWER, WILLIAM H. An introduction to the osteology of the mammalia. 3d ed. London: Macmillan & Co., 1885.

HYMAN, LIBBIE H. Comparative vertebrate anatomy. 2d ed. Chicago: University of Chicago Press, 1942.

JAYNE, HORACE. Mammalian anatomy, Part I: The skeleton of the cat. Philadelphia: J. B. Lippincott Co., 1898.

MIVART, ST. GEORGE J. The cat. New York: Charles Scribner's Sons, 1881.

MORRIS, SIR HENRY. Human anatomy. Edited by BARRY J. ANSON. 2d ed. New York: Blakiston Div. McGraw Hill, 1966.

NEAL, HERBERT V., and RAND, HERBERT W. Chordate anatomy. Philadelphia: Blakiston Co., 1939.

———. Comparative anatomy. Philadelphia: Blakiston Co., 1936.

PEPPER, O. H. PERRY. Medical etymology. Philadelphia: W. B. Saunders Co., 1949.

RANSON, STEPHEN W. and CLARK, S. L. The anatomy of the nervous system. 10th ed. Philadelphia: W. B. Saunders Co., 1959.

REIGHGARD, JACOB E., and JENNINGS, H. S. Anatomy of the cat. Edited by RUSH ELLIOTT. 3d ed. New York: Holt, Rinehart and Winston, 1935.

SOBOTTA, JOHANNES. Atlas of human anatomy. Edited by J. PLAYFAIR MCMURRICH from 6th German ed. 3 vols. New York: G. E. Stechert & Co., 1927–30.

WALKER, WARREN F. A study of the cat. Philadelphia: W. B. Saunders Co., 1967.

WEICHER, CHARLES K. Representative chordates. New York: McGraw-Hill, 1961.

INDEX

[Boldface numbers refer to plates; other numbers refer to the pages opposite the plates and to the pages of the Glossary.]

ganglia. See sympathetic ganglia, 65
notch, **2,** 2, **3,** 67
vein, **45, 52,** 52
Vertebrarterial foramen. See transverse foramen 66
Vesicular
    artery, 50
    follicle. See ovarian follicle, 63
Vestibular ganglion, 8, 67
Vestibule of vagina, **40,** 40, 67
Vestibulocochlear nerve, 8, **56,** 56, 67
Vestigial, 67

Visceral
    arches, 5, 67
    branch of a spinal nerve. See communicating
        branch of spinal nerve, 59
    peritoneum, 33
    pleura, 43
    ramus of a spinal nerve. See communicating
        branch of spinal nerve, 59
    sensory paths, 46
    skeleton. See visceral arches, 67
Vocal fold, **53,** 53
Vomer bone, 5, **6, 8,** 8, **9, 10,** 10

Vulva, 40, 67

White matter of nervous system, 54, 67
Womb. See uterus, 66

Xiphihumeralis muscle, **15, 17, 18, 19, 20,** 20, **21**
Xiphisternum. See xiphoid process, 67
Xiphoid
    cartilage, 4
    process, **1,** 1, **4,** 4, 67

Yolk sac, 35

Zygapophysis. See articular process
Zygomatic, 67
    arch, 5
    bone, **5,** 5, **6,** 67
        frontal process, **5, 6,** 67
        postorbital process. See zygomatic bone,
            frontal process.
    process of frontal bone, **5, 6, 7**
        of maxilla, **6**
        of temporal bone, **5, 6, 7**